The Joy of Jazz

Swing Era, 1935–1947

For Mae

Book design by Deborah Rich; cover design by Patty Maher.
Cover photograph of Benny Goodman and Lionel Hampton from Frank Driggs Collection.

Library of Congress Cataloging-in-Publication Data

Scanlan, Tom.
    The joy of jazz : Swing Era, 1935–1947 / Tom Scanlan.
        p.   cm.
    Discography: p.
    Includes bibliographical references and index.
    ISBN 1-55591-237-0 (pbk.)
    1. Swing (Music)—History and criticism.   2. Jazz—History and criticism.   3. Big band music—History and criticism.   I. Title.
    ML3518.S33   1996
    781.65'4—dc20   96-24981
                                                                     CIP
                                                                     MN

Printed in the United States of America
0 9 8 7 6 5 4 3 2 1

Fulcrum Publishing
350 Indiana Street, Suite 350
Golden, Colorado 80401-5093
(800) 992-2908 • (303) 277-1623

Contents

1

When Jazz Was Popular, and Why

2

White, Black, Brown, and Beige

3

Dozens of Great Players

Acknowledgments

Many thanks to:

Fulcrum senior editor Mark Carroll, a wise and delightful man who helped the author in countless ways. He knows a great deal about jazz music and also understands what makes the English language swing.

Fulcrum publicity whiz Sandy Trupp, who made this book possible by recommending me to Mark Carroll when he wanted to do a book on jazz.

Frank Driggs, jazz historian with a vast collection of photos, who loves melody as much as foot-stomping rhythm, and whose photos enliven this book considerably.

Down Beat magazine for permission to reprint old *Down Beat* covers. Permissions chief Tracey King was especially helpful.

My project editor at Fulcrum Publishing, Daniel Forrest-Bank, who has been quick to understand a septuagenarian's point of view and who has been enormously helpful in many ways.

George and Frances Ogg, whose computer and beyond-the-call computer assistance solved the challenging intricacies of preparing an index.

My most astute critic and editor for many decades, Mae Scanlan.

Preface

"So, we beat on, boats against the current, borne back ceaselessly into the past."
—Last sentence in *The Great Gatsby* by F. Scott Fitzgerald

Jazz music became an important part of my life as a teenager during the 1930s. Louis Armstrong, Fats Waller, Benny Goodman, Duke Ellington, Count Basie, and their colleagues on the bandstand, on radio, and in 78rpm record grooves, turned me on.

I was one of the white kids who was a regular patron of the black Howard Theater in my hometown, Washington, when the nation's capital city was segregated in most every way. At the Howard a different "name" black band could be heard every week for only thirty-five cents in the afternoon after school. The Basie band's first appearance at the Howard, in 1937 I think, remains one of my most exhilarating musical experiences ever.

From Ellington to Jimmie Lunceford, Chick Webb to Claude Hopkins, Earl Hines to the Mills Blue Rhythm Band, I heard them all at the Howard. Well, not Cab Calloway. Calloway's band was heard downtown. The singer fronted the only black band in those days able to appear at one of the two downtown white theaters with stage shows, the Earle and the Fox, where black people were not allowed to be in the audience. And it did not matter that many of us believed then, not easily by hindsight today, that it was infuriatingly absurd that skin color could keep anyone with the price of admission from enjoying Calloway's band at the Fox, or Teddy Wilson and Lionel Hampton with Goodman at the Earle.

Much of my early jazz education was at the Howard, but elsewhere in the city, "name" white bands, notably those led by Goodman and Artie Shaw, were heard at the Earle and Fox (this large, extraordinary theater was renamed the Capitol and eventually thoughtlessly demolished), and at such places as Uline Arena and Riverside Stadium, acoustical horrors built for ice skaters not for music. When Stan Kenton played at Uline he said he had not known his band would be playing in the Grand Canyon.

A Glenn Miller network broadcast was seen at the Wardman Park Hotel, and the Woody Herman band at Turner's Arena, usually used for boxing and wrestling matches, a rare place in town where black and white couples shared the dance floor. In Washington nightclubs I heard many jazz giants, in their prime, including Coleman Hawkins, Lester Young, Art Tatum, Billie Holiday, and Jack Teagarden. Once upon a time there was no constant fear of crime—fueled by heroin and later crack cocaine addiction—in my hometown and this was when there was much jazz to be enjoyed in Washington.

While more affluent kids may have been dancing to dull "mickey mouse" music at the Shoreham Hotel's Blue Room, I listened, transfixed, to the wondrous sounds of the Ellington and Lunceford bands in black dance halls and hotels where few white people were to be found. And social historians majoring in big-city Americana as it once was may be interested to know that I never heard a racial slur of any kind directed my way during any of my Swing Era nights at dances where whites were outnumbered fifty-to-one or at black jazz clubs where I always seemed welcome. I had no trouble then going anywhere in my hometown in search of exciting jazz music.

Trips to Atlantic City were made not to ride waves in the ocean but to hear, and dance to, the music of prominent swing bands in two ballrooms on ocean piers beside the boardwalk. Summer job money was saved not for an automobile but to make train trips to New York City for Fifty-second Street music clubs, Nick's in Greenwich Village, and other clubs and dance halls in Manhattan where jazz heroes worked. And to indicate how things were in those days, even when I was a high school student just beginning to shave I was never asked to show an ID card, for age, in order to listen and drink in those clubs.

Jazz record collecting was a constant activity. But it wasn't like collecting stamps or baseball cards. It wasn't done to own records, rare or not. Phonograph records were collected to play and enjoy. Some that were played over and over again—by Ellington, Goodman, Basie, Waller, Teddy Wilson with Billie Holiday—were not rare at all. As for so-called collector's items, some of my rare and therefore supposedly more valuable records—by Bessie Smith, Clarence Williams,

Jean Goldkette, and McKinney's Cotton Pickers—were found in used record stores and cost only five or ten cents.

During World War II Army service, before duty overseas, I heard decent small band jazz in clubs and danced to swing bands in ballrooms across the nation, from Miami to Wichita to Denver to Salt Lake City and Seattle, discovering that jazz is where you find it, not always where it's supposed to be according to *Down Beat*. Who was that blind trumpet player with the fat tone and great range in an unpretentious Miami Beach nightclub in 1943? I have no idea, but he could play!

Surely thousands of hours have been spent enjoying jazz in black and white nightclubs, in gin mills and fancy hotels, in gyms and concert halls, in after-hours clubs, and several times on a prison baseball field.

The Club Bengasi on Washington's U Street was my favorite club in the late 1940s until the owner took a sudden and sneaky flyer one morning, leaving Erroll Garner and others without pay for a week's work. (The place was carried for years on the lengthy national "defaulters" list of the American Federation of Musicians. About fifteen years after the owner took off, Garner told me, unsurprisingly, that he was never paid anything for that gig. You might say it was all part of the scuffling jazz life, the way it sometimes was and still is. It's easy to understand why some musicians insist upon being paid *before* the job. As for Garner's financial woes, they ended, and how, after Martha Glaser became his manager and he began to make big bucks.)

In contrast to New York, that city that "never sleeps," at one time all Washington nightclubs had to close by 2 A.M., and on Saturdays by midnight because of Sunday no-liquor laws. After-hours clubs therefore existed. In one of the half-dozen black after-hours clubs, Sarah Vaughan played piano for fun one morning, delighting one and all without singing a single note. In one of several white after-hours clubs, the nationally unknown but easily the best jazz accordion player I ever heard, Dick Bailey, worked regularly.

I went to prison, as guest not inmate, with Louis Armstrong, Count Basie's band, Stuff Smith, Oscar Peterson, Ramsey Lewis, Herb Ellis, Ella Fitzgerald, Charlie Byrd, among others, to watch them perform all-out at no charge for appreciative audiences on sweltering Washington summer days. As Ella sang a ballad, beautifully as was her habit on one such July afternoon, I recall an older trustee prisoner, whose temporary duty was to serve us lemonade in the prison field's baseball dugout, telling me correctly and softly, with moist eyes, "she sings like an angel."

This annual Lorton (prison) Jazz Festival began because of another singer, Sarah Vaughan, and a thoughtful prison chaplain, Father Carl Breitfeller. He had noticed one of the prisoners was a big Sarah Vaughan fan with many pictures of her in his cell. When the singer came to town for a week's engagement at a nightclub, the chaplain went to see if he could get an autographed picture for the prisoner. Sarah told him she could do better than that. "How about me bringing some musicians and singing at the prison?," she asked. That's how the festival began. Popular Washington jazz disc jockey Felix Grant attended these festivals for about 1,700 men every year. And many jazz fans kept asking him if there was any way they could get into the Lorton Jazz Festival. "I told them sure there's a way to get in," said Grant, "only it's not so easy to get out."

Although mainly involved with other newspaper work, I began to be called a jazz critic around 1952 because of my jazz column in *Army Times*, a national weekly newspaper with a substantial circulation, well over 200,000, although it was not seen by a great many civilians. A record producer once wisecracked that jazz critics were only guys who expect to get free records all the time, and maybe so, but getting hundreds of free "for review" 45s, LPs, and tapes year after year always seemed delightfully right and proper to me.

I do play guitar, but working gigs and sitting in with true professionals years ago taught me the great difference between amateur and professional. The real pros seem to know all the changes to virtually all the tunes, for one thing. And they can transpose (from one key to another) quickly and accurately. Maybe a good ear and a compulsion to swing can get you by on a horn but that isn't enough when you are playing chord changes on a guitar.

What with work off and on for a newspaper during five years of college, as a young man I could not—at least did not—give guitar the practice time required to become better than mediocre. (The education was made possible by that splendid piece of congressional legislation called the G.I. Bill of Rights, World War II version. In my case, it ended with a master's degree in English Literature and the writing bug stronger than ever.)

So I have always been jazz fan, not jazz musician. But my guitar playing, a smattering of harmony and theory instruction, and a knowledge of many old tunes and familiar chord progressions did help my writing on jazz. At least no one had to tell me that *Rachel's Dream* was based on *Three Little Words, Hot House* on *What Is This Thing Called Love?*, and *Lullaby of Birdland* on *Love Me or Leave Me*. I was also aware that Tal Farlow was remembering April when he played *And She Remembers Me*. As jazz musicians have known for decades, you should copyright a melody, but you can't copyright a chord progression.

Taste in music, musical ears, and accurate rhythmic time are not determined by whether one plays an instrument or not. But those who do play tend to be more appreciative of what some who don't play call "mere technical skill." Such skill involves proper notes in proper places, tone, range, dynamics, intonation. The old line, stated while tuning up, "it's close enough for jazz," is after all only a joke.

I wrote interview and opinion pieces, performance and book reviews for *Down Beat* as well as nearly 1,000 jazz columns for *Army Times*. During those years, twenty-five to forty years ago, I also wrote a fifty-six-program history of jazz for the Voice of America (VOA) and about 200 other jazz programs for the Voice. All of these half-hour programs were translated into many foreign languages for broadcast overseas. None was in English. (Willis Conover did VOA's English-speaking jazz programs for decades, introducing who knows how many thousands to the joys of this American music and no doubt a good many to the English language as well.)

I took part in *Down Beat*'s "International Jazz Critics Poll" for more than a dozen years, serving as a kind of minority voice, voting for nonwinners such as Ruby Braff, Clark Terry, Bobby Hackett, Joe Wilder, Zoot Sims, Teddy Wilson, Dave McKenna, Keter Betts, Urbie Green, Freddie Green, Joe Mooney, and many other exceptional players who received few votes. I also wrote LP liner notes for Washington musicians I knew and liked including pianist John Eaton and finger-style (no pick) guitarists Charlie Byrd and Bill Harris. Byrd and Harris both used their G.I. Bills to study with Washington's Sophocles Papas, a former Segovia student and at that time the only guitar teacher in the United States accredited to accept G.I. Bill payment. Papas refused to admit Harris at first, because of skin color, but Bill complained to the Veterans Administration. With the VA's assistance, Harris integrated Papas's guitar school.

Aside from occasional columns of appreciation for favorite players such as Hackett and Ben Webster and a few jazz book reviews for Washington daily newspapers, I made little time for jazz writing during my twelve years as editor of *Federal Times,* then a feisty tabloid called a critical watchdog of the federal bureaucracy, thanks to talented and determined young reporters who rushed in where others feared to tread. With my retirement from newspaper deadlines in 1985, there has been a return to writing about jazz. I was the writer for the memoirs of the late rhythm guitar master Steve Jordan (*Rhythm Man: Fifty Years in Jazz,* University of Michigan Press, 1991).

The book in your hand is in no way a definitive report on the Swing Era. It's closer to being what some contemporary newspaper people call an "overview." A critical bibliography suggesting some of the better books involving this exciting jazz period is included for anyone seeking further information. A selected discography is also here to help those who may want to hear some of the best music recorded during the Swing Era.

This book is not always politically or verbally correct. It may be a generational thing but as one who thinks being called "a print media person" is ridiculous, I write, for example, "heavy drinker," not "alcohol abuser." (And, to be sure, the Swing Era had its share of heavy drinkers.)

Nor is this book always critically correct if the yardstick is conventional critical wisdom. This is probably because of a reluctance to repeat popular but questionable opinions not my own. For example, this book does not embrace a fashionable Jazz History 101 idea that Lester Young and Charlie Christian were "precursors of bop." And this book no doubt reflects the author's view that despite all the important and ingenious jazz composers and arrangers, jazz is primarily a player's art, not a composer's art, another idea that is not exactly critically correct in some academic and quasi-academic quarters today.

The Swing Era is not pinned down nor summed up somewhat disparagingly as the Big Band Era in this book simply because memory insists, and recordings prove, the Swing Era was not just a Big Band Era but probably the greatest Small Band Era, too.

Unlike some professorial studies of the Swing Era, there is no attempt here to develop or search for an innovative thesis of import that, say, finds fascinating ways to link swing music to the politics, sociological problems, "culture" of the time, whatever. The emphasis here is on the marvelous and distinctively different jazz players of the Swing Era. Those who may think that jazz players tend to sound alike, are urged to discover Swing Era jazz.

An explanation of the years 1935–1947 in the subtitle of this book is probably necessary. Unlike declared wars, human lives, and presidential administrations, eras are not easily dated.

As for the Swing Era, it is easy to date the beginning, 1935, because of the astounding commercial success of the Benny Goodman orchestra that brought jazz surprisingly to center stage in late 1935. Jazz historians, as many jazz writers now like to describe themselves, don't agree on much, but most seem to agree on the year 1935 for the Swing Era's birth. But just when the Swing Era ended is primarily opinion.

Many, in and out of academe, find it neat and tidy to view most everything by decades—thus, "The Roaring Twenties" and, much earlier, "The Gay Nineties." Even some bright academics now find time to pontificate in print about the social changes wrought by sexual revolution, rock 'n' roll, and "The Fifties." But the Swing Era will not fit neatly into such a numerical decade. There was no Swing Era in 1930 and the Swing Era was riding high in 1940. Nor was it over by 1945, so even the years 1935–1945 won't do.

The year 1947 was chosen because in December 1946 prominent swing bands led by Woody Herman, Tommy Dorsey, Harry James, Jack Teagarden, Benny Carter, and Benny Goodman disbanded (some returned later), and in 1947 other touring bands and many local and area bands similarly called it quits as ballrooms and other places to play closed. In 1947, big band musicians who had recently returned from World War II service found job opportunities extremely limited, and even Swing Era solo stars scuffled for small band gigs as bebop became the jazz music of choice for hipper-than-thou jazz critics and younger jazz musicians who were swept up with the excitement of new sounds and wider harmonies to play with and upon.

Also, in 1947, Jimmie Lunceford, who led one of the great Swing Era bands, died of a heart attack in Seaside, Oregon, while on tour with a band that was only an imitation of his once delightful orchestra, a sad and perhaps symbolic end to the Swing Era.

But 1947 as the final year of the Swing Era is a circa date, not a firm date. The Swing Era did not end suddenly, as it more or less began. And many great Swing Era players certainly kept swinging for many years, some for more than several decades after 1947. Almost always, however, they played to a smaller and less receptive audience.

Forty years ago, one of my newspaper columns began: "Jazz is fun music that hooks you early in life and sticks with you." I still believe that. It has certainly stuck with me.

Jazz today seems more pretentious than it once was, much less joyful and more limited in melodic appeal, although honest exciting jazz can still be found here and there. But as jazz has diminished in quantity, originality, popularity, and availability, and as American popular music keeps dumbing down into bewildering new rock-bottom levels of monotony and vulgarity with no place at all for any would-be emulators of George and Ira Gershwin, Cole Porter, Irving Berlin, or Johnny Mercer, some of us who came of age during the Swing Era still beat on, boats against the current, snapping fingers to an old tune while measures of improvisation by some Swing Era player bounce around in brain and heart. And we are borne back persistently if not ceaselessly into the past.

The Joy of Jazz

Ellingtonians at Work—The Duke Ellington Band at the Hurricane Club in New York City, 1944. Players shown, from left to right, are Ellington at the piano, guitarist Freddie Guy, bassist Junior Raglin, tenor saxophonist Al Sears, drummer Sonny Greer, alto saxophonist Johnny Hodges, trombonist Joe "Tricky Sam" Nanton, clarinetist Jimmy Hamilton, trumpeter Sheldon Hemphill, and trombonist Claude Jones. (Copyright Frank Driggs Collection.)

1

When Jazz Was
Popular, and Why

*"At that time there were about twelve clubs between Fifth and Sixth
Avenues on Fifty-second Street. It was an exciting block ... . People
would go from one club to another and listen to jazz for five or six
hours. It was a way of life."*

—Bud Freeman

"The Swing Era," Woody Herman once recalled, rightfully, "was when jazz had the kids." And I remember those years well because I was one of the kids it had. For me and many others who are now septuagenarians, the title of a 1931 Duke Ellington ditty, *It Don't Mean a Thing If It Ain't Got That Swing,* was simply an obvious truth, a given, much like saying the sun sets in the west, or Art Tatum is a genius.

The Swing Era was when jazz was a major part of popular music. It is hardly even a minor part now. (Check cassette or compact disc sales charts, click on the television, or turn on the radio.) The Swing Era was when good musicians could find employment and sometimes even fame in big or small bands, and when dancing was a primary form of entertainment for adults as well as teenagers.

The Swing Era was when the immensely talented, highly skilled and charismatic pianist Fats Waller proved over and over again that he could really "turn it on," as he said, and make you laugh at the same time. ("No, lady, we can't haul your ashes for twenty-five cents, that's bad business ... yas, yas, yas, swing it on out! All right then!")

The Swing Era was when Billie Holiday was a stunning young woman to see as well as hear, when her singing was a rhythmic rush and her very sound a unique jazz instrument that could be played by only one person in the world.

The Duke Ellington orchestra, not the piano, was Ellington's major instrument, and the Swing Era was when this exceptional orchestra was at its absolute peak. This was when *Concerto for Cootie, Cottontail, Warm Valley, Dusk, All Too Soon, In a Mellotone,* and so many of the best Ellington pieces, were new. It was also when the addition of young composer-arranger Billy Strayhorn made Ellington's music even greater than it had been before.

The Swing Era was when Benny Goodman seemed infinitely more than a great clarinet player and rags-to-riches celebrity because he was a hero, a musician whose artistic and commercial success heroically opened the whole wide world of jazz to hundreds of thousands who had never heard of Benny Carter or Fletcher Henderson.

Born and bred in a Chicago ghetto, Goodman was also a new kind of hero because by hiring black musicians—"I'm selling music, not prejudice" was his terse explanation—he broke the entertainment color line more than a decade before Branch Rickey changed major league baseball by signing Jackie Robinson to play for the Brooklyn Dodgers. And Goodman did not do this as some kind of activist determined to alter and improve the social order, to help equalize liberty and the pursuit of happiness. He did it, warily at first, because he loved to play music with Teddy Wilson and Lionel Hampton, and because by nature he did not like people telling him what he could or could not do, especially when it involved music, his all-consuming passion as well as his profession since age thirteen.

The Swing Era was when the very word "Basie" first brightened the countenance of just about anyone who responded to jazz music, when the first Count Basie band set a new high standard for swinging. Many who heard that band agree with what Harry "Sweets" Edison, one of its most valuable players, said years later: "It was the greatest band that's ever been on earth! I've never heard any other band swing like it did."

The Swing Era was when nifty xylophonist Red Norvo was young and beardless, when he and jolly, hefty Mildred Bailey, whose clear-as-crystal voice was a true definition of lilt, were properly billed as

"Mr. and Mrs. Swing." The Swing Era was when Stuff Smith was proving that the proper way to play a violin was not the only way, and when a new instrument—the vibraphone, the vibraharp, or simply the vibes—became a marvelous rhythmic and melodic tool for jazz, thanks to Lionel Hampton.

Just as poets fool around with words, jazz musicians fool around with melodies, and the Swing Era was when ingenious melodizer Lester Young, "Pres," was at the top of his amazing melodic game, creating memorable melodies while cherishing familiar ones, with a tone like velvet. He was distinctively different from the great Coleman Hawkins and Hawk's many emulators. The Swing Era was when Lester Young was a jam session champion, as were easy-does-it trombonist Jack Teagarden, "Big Tea," and daredevil trumpet wizard Roy Eldridge, "Little Jazz."

The Swing Era was when men, and women too, wore hats and garters, and when musicians wore coats and ties on the handstand. It was also when good tap dancers were plentiful and great ones were not rare.

The Swing Era was when a no-smoking sign in a jazz club would have been unthinkable and when it seemed as if most adults smoked, usually Camel, Lucky Strike, or Chesterfield (no filters) and when these brands and others sponsored big band radio shows. Moving hard liquor "down the hatch" was also more prevalent than it is today, and the world of jazz had many players who could have competed in any heavy drinking championship tournament. (The majority of jazz musicians did not smoke marijuana but some did, including such famous players as Louis Armstrong and Lester Young. As did singer Billie Holiday, who—as is well known—moved on, and down, to heroin addiction.)

During Swing Era years, from the mid-1930s until roughly the late 1940s, jazz was not considered a problem to brood about nor did it pretend to rival Beethoven for profundity. It was fun, something to enjoy. For many people today, and for several decades now, jazz has seemed to be a precious, somewhat mysterious esoteric art form often divorced not only from popular song but from the proven verities of rhythm, melody, and harmony. It was decidedly not that during the Swing Era. Nor was it, as jazz has sometimes appeared to be in recent years, a philosophical viewpoint inspired by thoughts involving strong racial, sociological, even religious positions, or what was once called art for art's sake. Swing Era musicians did not pontificate, and they talked about music, not art. They did not think their work required aesthetic or philosophical explanation, but needed only good ears and an ability to keep time. "Jazz is pat your foot," said Count Basie, wisely. Swing Era musicians understood that jazz was most of all fun.

Today's jazz musicians do not play today's popular music, which is surely understandable, but jazz musicians did then. Swing Era jazz was deeply involved with the best popular music of the day, meaning new songs (now called "standards") written by men like Cole Porter, George Gershwin, Irving Berlin, Jimmy Van Heusen, Jerome Kern, Jimmy McHugh, Harold Arlen, and let's-not-forget Harry Warren, who is too often forgotten. Few of us who were jazz crazy during the Swing Era can begin to play or hum *I Can't Get Started* without thinking of how marvelously Bunny Berigan, a trumpet player's trumpet player, enriched this 1936 Vernon Duke song, shifting with ease from low to upper register while still maintaining tone, intonation, and immense power. Similarly, *Stars Fell on Alabama* and Harold Arlen's *I Gotta Right to Sing the Blues* were owned by Jack Teagarden, a thoroughly relaxed musician whatever the tune, tempo, or musical situation. Big Tea's right hand on the slide of what he liked to call his "trambone" seemed to move like jelly.

And when some of us hear *Embraceable You*, a 1930 Gershwin charmer, we think of golden-toned cornetist Bobby Hackett, a blacksmith's son from Providence, a one-time guitarist who never forgot passing chords, a man who never seemed to meet a man he didn't like nor a pleasant melody he could not make even more pleasing. The granddaddy of jazz on the tenor saxophone, Coleman Hawkins, knew exactly what to do with Richard Whiting's *My Ideal* or Johnny Green's *Body and Soul,* and Benny Goodman was quick to use such great then-new tunes as *Just One of Those Things* (Cole Porter, 1935) and *Where or When* (Richard Rodgers, 1937) for expert enhancement by his small groups. Countless other examples could be cited. After all, in those days anyway, jazz players needed decent songs to play because meandering around simple chord changes or indeed no chord changes at all, as favored by a jazz avant garde group decades later, would not have passed any kind of muster. Not even Count Basie players wanted to play the blues or rhythm chord progressions all night. And it might be mentioned that what jazz players still refer to as "rhythm" or the "rhythm progression" comes directly from the chord changes on Gershwin's *I Got Rhythm* (and perhaps Gershwin

8

heard these changes being used by jazz players before he wrote them down, who knows?).

Ellington was almost always busy playing Ellington or the work of his superb composing collaborator Billy Strayhorn, not standards from the 1920s or the popular music of the day. But most all other major jazz performers of the Swing Era leaned heavily on songs written not for jazz musicians but for Broadway, the movies (where Harry Warren was a champion), or what was left (not much) of a dying Tin Pan Alley (sheet music sales went down as the radio and phonograph replaced the parlor piano). And did the master of American popular song, Irving Berlin, like the way Fletcher Henderson arranged Berlin's *Blue Skies* for the Goodman band, with that loud, brassy intro denoting, Fletcher joked, a storm before the blue skies arrive? A sure bet is that Berlin did not. In any event, the thirty-two-measure popular song was useful, almost essential grist for a Swing Era player's mill. Few wanted to play dull, old hat, dreary simplistic stuff such as *Tin Roof Blues*. It was much more interesting to see what could be done with, say, Harry Warren's *Jeepers Creepers*. Warren, a New Yorker who was originally Salvatore Guaranga, a man who adored the music of Puccini, and who had written such hits as *Rose of the Rio Grande*, *Nagasaki*, and *I Found a Million Dollar Baby in a Five and Ten Cent Store* before moving to Hollywood in 1932, once said that "here in Hollywood a songwriter was always the lowest form of animal life." Swing Era musicians did not share such a Hollywood point of view.

It should also be remembered that the jazz music of the Swing Era, whether played by big bands or small groups, reached out to its audience. Jazz was involved with song and dance, and the essential thing was communication with listeners as well as with other musicians on the bandstand, not mere egoistic self-expression. It had more of an "us" than "me" feeling, since swinging with and for other people was what it was all about.

Swinging. Some jazz slang expressions denote what cannot be described as well in more proper English, and the words *swing* and *swinging* are good examples. Charlie Byrd had it right when he said this during a roundtable discussion with other guitarists: "People accuse musicians of not knowing how to speak the language and of being illiterate, but take a word such as *swinging*. Among the four of us [three accomplished guitarists and me], the word *swinging* tells more of what we're talking about than any other word we can think of, right? A good many slang expressions are this way. They apply to something that is vague, but they relay a whole lot of information."

Indeed. And the best definition of *swinging* remains an aural one. You recognize it when you hear it. For example, listen to a recording of the original Basie band playing *One O'clock Jump*. It *swings* and notice that it is not a fast tempo. Swinging has never been a matter of allegro, or "up" tempo, as hundreds of other Swing Era recordings can prove. Nor is it merely a one-two-three-four steady rhythmic pulse, being much more than that. Some of the greatest Swing Era players, including Goodman, had a habit of playing on top of the beat, not speeding but pushing the rhythm of it all. *Swinging*, you might say. And one thing is certain: many important essentials and nuances of music can be learned with a good ear, persistent practice, and good teaching perhaps, but no one can teach anyone else how to *swing*.

Swing bands did have the kids during the Swing Era. But the era involved thousands who were not rhythm-crazed teenagers jitterbugging in saddle shoes and in the process promoting previously scuffling jazz musicians into celebrities. The Swing Era had many adults in its grip, too. They danced, drank, and let the good times roll in hotel ballrooms and new large nightclubs made possible by the repeal of Prohibition, which finally ended in December 1933. (No more bathtub gin! No more exploding homemade beer in the basement! No more somebody-sent-me pleas through peepholes to enter so-called "illegal" speakeasies!) And as jazz, under its new label "swing," began to receive a smattering of attention and understanding in magazines and newspapers, many adults who had been told that Paul Whiteman and George Gershwin had somehow made a "lady" out of jazz, now began to understand, if only faintly, that Louis Armstrong was the true king of jazz in the 1920s, not Whiteman, and that Armstrong had made a man, not a lady, out of jazz. At the same time some discovered that the real "jazz singer" was also this black man Armstrong, not the appealing show biz champion Al Jolson in blackface on one knee belting out *Mammy*.

Swing did bother and bewilder some quick to grumble that the music was too loud. Where, they asked, were the violins, and why in the world doesn't the leader use a baton? But it also bewitched many long past their teens. The idea that jazz, swing, whatever one chose to call this lowbrow musician's music, was exciting as well as important and truly American music began to seep into the ken of middlebrow and highbrow folk. Some upper-crusters took notice when

Leopold Stokowski, the somewhat Olympian conductor of the great Philadelphia Orchestra at the Academy of Music, praised Ellington and other jazz people and insisted he, too, was a jazz fan.

Life, the enormously popular picture magazine reportedly conceived by dramatist and politician Clare Boothe Luce—famous wife of its publisher Henry Luce—that outsold even his older *Time,* had a big spread on the Goodman band swinging in the Hotel Pennsylvania's Madhattan Room in a 1937 "*Life* Goes to a Party" feature. *Esquire,* the big (over ten by thirteen inches with many pages), expensive (fifty cents!), cartoon-laden monthly graced by such writers as F. Scott Fitzgerald, Ernest Hemingway, John Dos Passos, Erskine Caldwell, and its famous airbrushed strong-thighed Petty Girl, began to include good essays on jazz. Even *The New Republic,* specializing in literary and political criticism, had a first-class writer, Otis Ferguson, regularly extolling the joys of jazz.

Dorothy Baker's 1938 novel *Young Man With a Horn,* suggested by the life of Bix Beiderbecke, was a best-seller (and later was made into a miserable movie). Baker got the title from Ferguson's 1936 "Young Man With a Horn" *New Republic* appreciation of Beiderbecke, a heavy drinker and wondrous cornet player who died in 1931 at age twenty-eight and became a kind of jazz martyr.

A young Frenchman, Hugues Panassié, wrote *Le Jazz Hot* in 1934, and its 1936 version in English, *Hot Jazz,* received much attention. By 1939, as Otis Ferguson noted, this book had become "a standard source of extremely valuable misinformation."

College campuses had "hot clubs" of jazz record collectors, and many musicians and jazz fans read the glossy-papered tabloid *Down Beat,* which began publication in Chicago in 1934, just in time for the Swing Era. "The Beat," as many called it, was large and lively then. The magazine's jazz criticism was usually of the thumbs-up or thumbs-down variety, but the opinions and reports of George Frazier, Helen Oakley, and John Hammond were usually well worth reading. And George Hoefer's "Hot Box" of detailed discographical information was must-reading for jazz crusaders intent upon discovering just who played what brief solo on rare jazz records of the 1920s. *Down Beat* had lots of photos of prominent and mainly obscure female band "vocalists," also known as "canaries," frequently with skirts hiked high, plus snappy headlines such as: "I Saw Pinetop Spit Blood and Fall" (Pinetop Smith was an almost legendary boogie-woogie pianist who died in 1928), and "BG Pays Pianist 2 Weeks Salary for 3 Numbers" (a new pianist was fired by Benny Goodman after only one set, a happening that *Down Beat* proclaimed was "one of the goofiest stunts the King had yet pulled." Musicians read *Down Beat* for trade news and to find out where and with whom friends were playing. Jazz fans read *Down Beat* for information about new musical heroes and new recordings. The *Beat* also had classified ads, including an "At Liberty" section which often contained those then seemingly immortal words "have tux, will travel." Musicians dressed up, not down, then.

There were other jazz publications, but *Down Beat*'s only real competition came from the much less extensive *Metronome*, a rather sedate music magazine that was not sedate after switching enthusiastically to jazz and big bands when swing swung in. It included reviews and commentary by George Simon and a young Englishman who was to become one of the most prolific jazz critics, Leonard Feather, still adding to his millions of words on the subject when he died in 1994 at age eighty. During the Swing Era, movie stars dominated entertainment news overwhelmingly, but jazz musicians were not without considerable publicity. Goodman was certainly not the only jazz player who had to escape mobs of autograph hounds. (Goodman sometimes escaped crowds at stage doors simply by taking his glasses off.)

The Swing Era is known to many today as the Big Band Era, "big band" at that time meaning an orchestra of thirteen to fifteen musicians, usually, plus a singer or two. During the 1930s and early 1940s, in addition to local bands and "territory bands" that toured in only one area of the country, dozens of "name bands" or would-be name bands criss-crossed the nation by auto, bus, and train to play music in nightclubs, hotels, movie theaters, ballrooms, National Guard armories, country clubs, boxing arenas, college gyms, and on seashore amusement piers. Indeed, touring big bands were booked most anywhere there was a dance floor, including riverboats with early "moonlight" and later "midnight" dance cruises.

In the forty-eight United States, there were hundreds of ballrooms. These were in cities large and small. Younger readers can ask grandparents where such ballrooms used to be. Extremely few still exist.

Most of the touring bands were swing bands, but some of these were boring musically with sloppy section work and wavering intonation. They often featured attractive young female singers who lost considerable attractiveness when they tried to sing. Such bands served mainly as a beat for jitterbugs to lindy hop or shag to. But a rising tide lifts all ships, so such mediocre bands, black and white, could make it too, more or less. There were also orchestras on tour that did not swing, could not swing, and had no desire to swing. And a few of these so-called "sweet music" bands had what many swing bands, weary of endless one-nighters, yearned to have: long engagements in prominent hotels. Two Manhattan examples were Guy Lombardo's orchestra, seriously billed as producing "The Sweetest Music This Side of Heaven" at the Hotel Roosevelt, and Vincent Lopez's similar group of businessmen music makers at the Hotel Taft. It is understandable why jazz histories seldom include their existence, but name bands led by baton-wielders Lombardo, Sammy Kaye, Shep Fields (who actually, believe it or not, blew through a straw into a small bowl of water to get his famous "rippling rhythm"), and Blue Barron were decidedly on the scene and at least commercially successful. Lombardo made much more money than Louis Armstrong.

These "sweet" bands had one advantage, perhaps: not all who went out dancing could keep good rhythmic time, so dancing to such "ricky tick" hotel bands enabled the rhythmically challenged to create their own time, more or less, a happening that would have been viewed as ludicrous if attempted to the music of a swing band with "a solid beat."

Largely because of radio, Lombardo led the most famous of all the "schmaltz" bands. It was reported that by 1942 Lombardo had grossed over $2 million from radio and over $1 million from hotels, BIG money then. But Blue Barron's band, not Lombardo's, won all the marbles for being the antithesis of hip, stressing purposely saccharine sounds that included hiccuping muted trumpets, whining saxophones with pulsing vibratos, and assorted unbelievably inane, cutesy, corn-ball tricks. Proving the sanity of poet Alexander Pope's observation that all looks yellow to the jaundiced eye, Barron wrote a 1941 piece for the magazine *Music & Rhythm* stating that swing was "nothing but orchestrated sex," obviously suggesting there was nothing sexy about his music, and there wasn't. In 1942, another Barron essay predicted that "sweet musicians will be able to play at the funeral of swing." That did not happen.

Jazz musicians and their fans called sweet orchestras "sissy" or "mickey mouse" bands, and no remembrance of the Swing Era would be complete without their mention, also serving to remind us that all God's chillun, then as now, do not have rhythm. Charlie Barnet, the blithe spirit who led one of the more successful swing bands, satirized mickey mouse bands, hilariously, on a recording entitled *The Wrong*

Idea that Sammy Kaye, for one, did not find funny. Barnet said Kaye refused to speak to him for years because of this record. Such a reaction by Kaye may have been partly due to *The Wrong Idea*'s subtitle: *Swing and Sweat With Charlie Barnet*. This was an obvious reference to how Kaye's band was billed: "Swing and Sway with Sammy Kaye," as if swing had anything to do with Kaye's music. The other side of this Barnet record on Victor's thirty-five-cent Bluebird label—78rpm, as were all records then—was *The Right Idea,* which aimed to acknowledge the rightness of Ellington harmonies and Basie swing.

But despite Lombardo and his emulators, most big bands of the period were peopled by musicians who were inspired by the great jazz musicians of the time, as were those often unheralded men (and a few women, notably pianist Mary Lou Williams and four-foot-eleven Margie Gibson) who wrote orchestrations for the best swing bands including those of Goodman and Basie.

Too many jazz history books present the Swing Era as the Big Band Era, period, explaining that small band jazz moved in with bop in the late 1940s. Those who write such misleading books can say it over and over again—Big Band Era, Big Band Era—but the truth is that the Swing Era was a many-splendored world of jazz activity, not just a Big Band Era. Small band jazz of a high order was as vigorous and ubiquitous as big band jazz. Jazz or "swing" combos of three to seven pieces were to be found not only in those narrow clubs with small bandstands on West Fifty-second Street where jazz masters mesmerized other musicians and true believers, but in similar smoky drinking places in countless cities across the nation.

The Reno Club in Kansas City at Twelfth and Cherry was one such example. Beer was five cents, hot dogs a dime, imported Scotch fifteen cents, and—of major importance to music lovers—a nine-piece Count Basie group worked long hours for peanuts for two years. This was before Basie and his colleagues swung at the Roseland Ballroom in Manhattan (where be-gowned partners were no longer ten cents a dance but $1.80 an hour), at the "Home of Happy Feet" Savoy Ballroom and Apollo Theater in Harlem, at Fifty-second Street's Famous Door, and as this Washingtonian will never forget—at the Howard Theater in Washington.

John Hammond, son of a Vanderbilt and a never-say-die fighter for jazz as well as desegregation before such fighting was fashionable, had gone to the Reno Club in 1936 to hear Basie and rapidly became the man who moved the pianist and his musicians from this Kansas

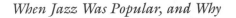

More Than Ten Cents a Dance—New York's Famous Roseland Ballroom in 1936, the year a new band led by Woody Herman made it big there on election night. Notice signs proclaiming "continuous dancing" in a "cool, comfortable, spacious" place with "hostesses" to dance with. By 1936, such dancing partners cost more than a dime a dance. (Copyright Frank Driggs Collection.)

City joint (where Basie made eighteen dollars a week) to national attention. And all this came about because Hammond happened to hear Basie's band from the Reno Club on a Kansas City station on his car radio while in Chicago with Goodman.

It may amaze younger radio listeners to know that fifty-some years ago it was easy to find exciting jazz on the radio. There were many good bands, large and small, to be heard on some local stations and on the Mutual, CBS, and two NBC (red and blue) radio networks. Radio "remotes" so called because they were not from broadcast studios but from a remote place, certainly made some bands famous. Many bands were willing to work for less than their usual wage if their place of employment had network radio remotes.

For a new band, radio remotes were probably more important for success than a hit recording, although a single hit record could certainly help to "make" a band. To list a few such hits: Artie Shaw's *Begin the Beguine,* Charlie Barnet's *Cherokee,* Woody Herman's *Woodchopper's Ball,* and Glenn Miller's *In the Mood.* The last one was written by Joe Garland, veteran saxophonist with prominent black bands, who began to earn substantial royalties on this big hit years later, only after joining ASCAP.

Complete with chatter from the dancers and listeners where the bands were playing, I remember hearing Fats Waller broadcasting from the Panther Room at the Hotel Sherman in Chicago, and dozens of different bands from Frank Dailey's Meadowbrook in Cedar Grove, New Jersey, the Marine Ballroom at the rear of the long Steel Pier in Atlantic City, the Palomar Ballroom in Los Angeles, the Raymor Ballroom in Boston, the Trianon Ballroom in Chicago, and many places in New York, including the Famous Door, the Savoy Ballroom, and the Hotels Edison, Lincoln, Pennsylvania, and New Yorker. And there were radio remotes from many other cities. Such broadcasts, each usually a half-hour in length and most one after another from 11 P.M., sometimes earlier, seven days a week, also served as dance music for Saturday night neighborhood parties in cities large and small. People of all ages danced, together not apart, and in their homes with the rugs rolled up (wall-to-wall carpeting was yet to come), with music from the radio or the phonograph, those marvelous instruments that had replaced the parlor piano. To dance, it wasn't necessary to "go out."

The Swing Era was deeply involved with dancers. It should not be forgotten, as some who have written jazz history books seem to forget or never knew, that Benny Goodman led a *dance* band. And so did all the leaders of all the swing bands. Many may think of *Sing, Sing, Sing* or *Bugle Call Rag* when Goodman is mentioned, but the tempo for, say, *Estrellita,* or the popular *Don't Be That Way,* was more typical of the Goodman orchestra. Most of his music was played at a most danceable, lively but medium tempo. This included, even, *Star Dust,* which was customarily played much slower by other bands. Goodman, like other successful swing band leaders, had the dancers. And when jazz lost the dancers, it lost the ballrooms and most all of the big bands. The extremely slow tempo favored by Stan Kenton for ballads was not favored by the swing bands that preceded Kenton.

During the Swing Era, a buck or less would get you into a ball-room. There you could dance a simple box step or something similar to the fox trot of the 1920s which moved you around the entire dance floor and let you dream you were gliding as gracefully as Fred Astaire. And there was the bouncier, twirl-your-partner lindy hop, which became known as jitterbugging. (Yes, the lindy hop, created in Harlem, was named for Lindbergh's famous Atlantic Ocean solo flight, or hop, to Paris in 1927.) The shag, repeated quick up-and-down steps, was also popular. And if you had no dancing partner, you sim-ply listened to the call-and-response patterns of the reed and brass sections, enlivened by soloists "taking off," which meant improvis-ing, more or less. Tommy Dorsey had a superb trombone sound and was matchless on ballads, but for jazz excitement we waited for Dorsey's trumpet powerhouse Bunny Berigan or tenor saxophonist Bud Freeman to solo. Andy Kirk meant solos by pianist Mary Lou Williams and tenor man Dick Wilson. Almost every decent swing band had a few jazz stars, and some, including one fronted by a singer, Bing Crosby's younger brother Bob, had many. Jimmy Dorsey, on clarinet as well as alto sax, was the star of his own band but Tommy's slightly older brother had other able soloists, notably tenor saxo-phonist Herbie Haymer, who was to become one of many Swing Era musicians killed in automobile crashes.

Driving at night after a one-nighter was one of the perils of being a big band musician. Two hundred musicians were killed or injured in a two-year period, according to a 1941 survey by the magazine *Music & Rhythm.* Musicians habitually traveled 250 to 600 miles a night after a one-nighter and road tours ranged from one month to six months. Trains were no solution because there were many ballrooms and clubs where trains did not go. In addition to those killed and seriously injured, there were many accidents that could have resulted in death. For example, in April 1941, three members of the Tommy Dorsey band as well as the wife of one "miraculously escaped being killed," according to *Down Beat,* when their auto crashed as they were making a one-nighter "jump" from Atlantic City to Binghamton, New York. The car rolled over twice and was totally demolished. Such stories were not uncommon in *Down Beat* during the Swing Era. Remember, too, that Atlantic City to Binghamton was not a short drive, particularly then, with no super highways. But it was the kind of one-nighter trip expected even if you were a musician skilled enough to be working in one of the truly "big name" bands such as Tommy Dorsey's.

1935, When Swing Swung In

In 1935, the nation was beginning to nurse its way out of the Great Depression that followed the stock market crash of 1929. The soul-searing Depression was a time of record unemployment, long bread lines, and hobo jungles. Lyricist Yip Harburg summed it up neatly in *Brother, Can You Spare a Dime?*, a 1932 hit song that had nothing to do with moon and June, dance and romance, and related customary subjects of popular song.

In 1935, President Franklin D. Roosevelt was creating a large number of new federal agencies, and social security legislation passed Congress. Republicans enjoyed newspaper columnists who railed against FDR's "New Deal" while Democrats were charmed by FDR's "fireside chats" on the radio.

The trial of Bruno Richard Hauptmann for the kidnap-murder of the Lindbergh baby created banner headlines, popular comic performer and homespun philosopher Will Rogers was killed in a plane crash in Alaska, and ambitious share-the-wealth demagogue Huey Long—Louisiana's "Kingfish"—was gunned down in Baton Rouge. Hitler ranted on about Nordic superiority and "the master race" as he rearmed Germany. Mussolini prepared to invade defenseless Ethiopia. There was much in print about "war clouds." And Hitler may not have noticed when non-Nordic Jesse Owens broke five track and field records on one 1935 day while tuning up for the 1936 Olympics in Berlin, an event Owens dominated, to Hitler's chagrin.

Porgy and Bess, described by composer George Gershwin as "a folk opera," opened in New York. Veteran song-and-dance-man Fred Astaire sang he was "in heaven" dancing *Cheek to Cheek* with Ginger Rogers in the smash hit movie *Top Hat* (music by Irving Berlin), and a baby named

A Swinging Couple—Mr. and Mrs. Tommy Dorsey, on the May 1, 1943, cover of Down Beat. *(Reprinted with permission from* Down Beat *magazine.)*

Elvis Presley was born in Tupelo, Mississippi. Also, that year, 1935, the Swing Era stomped in with Benny Goodman front and center.

The birth of the Swing Era is usually dated August 21, 1935. That was Goodman's opening night at the huge Palomar Ballroom in Los

Angeles, the night the Goodman band, after a year of struggle, not only made it but made it big, with fans standing and cheering around the bandstand. The Palomar engagement was extended for three weeks as Goodman set attendance records, playing a hard-driving brand of music foreign to most white ears. The band had bombed on a tour from New York, especially at the Trocadero Ballroom at Elitch Gardens in Denver. Hostesses got a dime for three dances there and management insisted that Goodman play some waltzes and cut out the noise. Benny was ready to disband, disgusted that his music was all but ignored while Kay Kyser's corny band, with funny hats on, drew large crowds nearby.

Although Goodman's band had managed, barely, to wangle a job as one of the three bands on the weekly *Let's Dance* program on NBC and sales of Goodman Trio and band recordings had been encouraging (including the Trio's *After You've Gone* and *Body and Soul*, and the band's *Sometimes I'm Happy* and *King Porter Stomp*), the Goodman orchestra was certainly not a success until the Palomar gig.

As saxophone player Art Rollini, in his 1987 autobiography, remembered about one of the band's first major failures: "We opened directly at the Roosevelt Hotel, following Guy Lombardo. Although we had quite a few ballad-type charts in our library, and I warned Benny to take it easy and play softly, he paid no heed and barreled into *King Porter Stomp* at the dinner hour. The management had never heard anything like this before. The waiters were rattling dishes, knives and forks, and holding their fingers in their ears. As a result we played there for only two weeks. We received two weeks' notice on the first night!"

Fletcher Henderson's arrangement of *King Porter Stomp* and similar it's-definitely-not-Lombardo music was, however, well received at MacFadden's ballroom in Oakland and at the much larger Palomar in L.A. (well under a buck to get in, and dinner for ninety cents). At the Palomar, crowds around the bandstand seemed familiar with Goodman's music, no doubt partly because one of the first musically aware disc jockeys, Al Jarvis, had been plugging Benny's music on his L.A. *Make Believe Ballroom* program. The Goodman band then moved on to Chicago's Congress Hotel, remained for months, and someone decided to call Benny "The King of Swing." He did not like the idea, went along with it reluctantly, began to accept it, and eventually seemed to enjoy his famous appellation. Artie Shaw, the most admired and most famous clarinetist of the Swing Era not named Benny Goodman, was billed as "The King of the Clarinet," which may or may not have amused Benny Goodman.

There had certainly been good large jazz bands before Goodman, such as those led by Ellington and Henderson, but there had been no large white jazz band comparable to Goodman's. Glen Gray and his Casa Loma Orchestra and the Dorsey Brothers Orchestra probably came closest, but they were stiff in comparison to the band Goodman led. Benny and company were in another, "more swinging" field of activity. The Henderson band had disbanded the same year Goodman started his band, one reason why Benny was able to hire Fletcher to write orchestrations. Fletcher's arrangements were a major reason for the band's success, but the Goodman band was exceptional also because Goodman was a holy terror for constant rehearsal and a relentlessly tough guy about getting music played precisely the way he wanted it. He had no patience for sloppy playing. And no white band and few black bands had a jazz soloist to match the major soloist in Benny's band, the clarinetist.

Before Goodman's success, white jazz fans were a small but devout group. Most white people knew little if anything about the music of Henderson, Ellington, or most any jazz musician. If they had heard of Ellington it was as one who played "jungle music" for "copper colored" dancers at the Cotton Club in Harlem, where blacks performed before white audiences, and possibly as the composer of *Sophisticated Lady*. They did know about Paul Whiteman's orchestra and singers Bing Crosby (who began as one of the singing "Rhythm Boys" with Whiteman), Al Jolson, and Gene Austin, the jaunty tenor who was the best-selling phonograph-record performer during the 1920s. They had heard of Louis Armstrong, perhaps, and Ethel Waters, maybe, but probably not great blues singer Bessie Smith. And if they "knew" any brass player ever with the Whiteman band it was apt to be Henry "Hot Lips" Busse, not Bix Beiderbecke. The kind of orchestra leaders most white people "knew" were not jazz players but singers such as Rudy Vallee ("my time is your time," he sang nasally) or Ted Lewis ("is everybody happy?"), nonmusicians such as gleeclub specialist Fred Waring and Ben Bernie ("yowsah!"), and because he led the orchestra on the popular Jack Benny comedy half-hour on radio, Don Bestor. Only the more musically aware "knew" Jean Goldkette, who led one of the best bands of the late 1920s, and Isham Jones, a great 1920s song writer (*On the Alamo, I'll See You in My Dreams* and the classic they-don't-write-songs-like-that-anymore *It Had to Be You*), from whose band Woody Herman sprung.

21

Benny Goodman changed public thinking about dance band musicians, popular music, jazz, and orchestra leaders, who suddenly needed no baton. His success put jazz musicians up front where they had seldom been before. As drummer Gene Krupa—a big star with the first Goodman band, who left persistent drummer-critic Goodman in 1938 because of personal and musical differences and quickly organized his own band—said years later: "Benny built himself a band playing musician's music. It allowed us to play the way we honestly wanted to play, with good pay and before huge, appreciative audiences. In the days before the Goodman era, we played that way, too, but in smaller bands and with no similar success, or in sessions held in empty halls with no one to appreciate our efforts but the fellows playing the other instruments. For all that Benny did for music, for jazz, for musicians, and for me, I for one doff my cap in a salute of sincere appreciation."

The Goodman era. Interesting that Krupa said that. A piano-playing friend of mine told me in 1939 that we were living in what would someday be called the Goodman era. And what is now known as the Swing Era could have been so named because Goodman was certainly the period's central figure. It was no surprise when he ran away with *Down Beat*'s annual "best soloist" polls. In recent years, some jazz history revisionists have downgraded Goodman's importance, even his amazing, often exquisite and heartfelt playing, but they seem entitled more to pity and censure than to approbation. Would there have been a Swing Era without Goodman? Perhaps. Would Goodman have been a famous jazz player if he had never led a band? Of course. Listen to him play. In any event, it was the success of the Goodman band that turned the popular music world upside down and decidedly for the better. Call it a kind of musician's revenge because jazz musicians, in the Swing Era, began to make more money than most of the square bandleaders they had sometimes been forced to work for, in order to eat, before swing arrived.

With Goodman's success, hot jazz musicians realized they need not be trapped in some kind of artistic limbo. They, too, could be financially successful playing the kind music they liked. They no longer had to work for peanuts in crummy joints or in boring "icky" bands while getting musical kicks in backroom jam sessions. In one year alone, 1939, more than a dozen jazz players who had gained fame as star swing band sidemen organized bands they hoped would become name bands, including Harry James, Teddy Wilson, Bob Zurke, Georgie Auld, and Wilbur Schwichtenberg. Those led by James and

Schwichtenberg did become prominent name bands. And if Wilbur Schwichtenberg does not sound familiar it is because he became Will Bradley when he was told his real name would not always fit on a marquee or in a headline, as it wouldn't.

Thirty-odd years after Teddy Wilson helped to create Swing Era history in more ways than one, as trio and quartet pianist with Goodman, as the first black to be featured with a white band in public, Wilson said this about those Swing Era years: "It was a very exciting period. The Goodman band was the first jazz to become a nationally popular thing, and it took us all by surprise. No one expected it."

The soft-spoken pianist, an articulate intellectual who was the son of an English professor at Tuskegee, said the Goodman band had "good intonation in the reed section, first-rate trumpet work, other musical values, and it was playing within the dance tradition."

Stressing that the band's success was tied up with dancing, he added: "Goodman would sometimes stand in front of the band tapping his foot for as long as a minute, almost as if feeling the pulse of the dancers, to assure the proper time."

Years later, Benny told his sterling lead trumpet player Jimmy Maxwell: "The tempo is the tempo you can sing the words to comfortably." The idea was that you should not play a song faster than you could sing it. Of course this had nothing to do with such Goodman up-tempo "killer dillers," as was said then, as *Bugle Call Rag*, which was not sung. And Benny must have forgotten his rule when he played *The World Is Waiting for the Sunrise* with pianist Mel Powell at a blistering tempo considerably quicker than "up."

Powell was a star with Goodman at age eighteen, long before he became a composer of formal modern music and a Pulitzer Prize winner. And few have explained as well as Powell what it was like to be about fourteen and hearing Goodman's band for the first time. Some of the best writing about jazz music is not in books but on record album liner notes, and Powell's memories of his first Goodman experience is a fine example. It comes from a 1988 liner note for an LP produced by the Yale Music Library, where the Goodman Archives are located. Recalling that he had been preparing "for what was expected to be a career as a concert pianist" and "had never heard jazz before, possibly had never heard of it," Powell wrote:

One day my younger brother persuaded our parents that he and I must be given appropriate financial subvention (approximately

$1.50, I think) to get from our apartment in the Bronx to seats in the Paramount Theater. There we would meet up in person with something spectacular he'd heard on the radio. A "King of Swing" was playing some kind of incredible music with a big band that ... incredible, incredible, he said, he simply couldn't describe it.

Neither can I today. But I can remember vividly that moment in the Paramount Theater when, with a boring movie finally having come to its end, the stage began slowly to rise up from darkness and soon turned into a celestial proscenium as spotlights started to glow—a singularly radiant vision brimming with the sparkle of big luminous cymbals and golden bells of horns—and suddenly there came forth a sound that in sheer vitality and splendor, in its stunning, ecstatic roaring, exceeded all previously known sonic delights by so immeasurably great a margin that ... but then, who can describe it?

That was the first time I saw and heard Benny Goodman. There must be extant nowadays a population of zillions of persons who did not see and hear Benny Goodman and his orchestra, or the trio with Benny, Teddy Wilson, and Gene Krupa, expanded to the quartet with Lionel Hampton, further expanded later to the various BG sextets, when he, they, "swing," and the world were young. I take it as axiomatic that each one of those zillions who missed it was born at the wrong time, possibly in the wrong place; in any event all of them are to be consoled as one consoles the bereft and the disenfranchised.

Powell expresses what so many of us felt upon first hearing Goodman. At about the same time he saw Goodman at the Paramount (where Benny had them dancing in the aisles), I was first seeing him at the Earle Theater in Washington. Like Mel, I am glad I was not born too late.

George Frazier, perhaps the best *writer* writing about jazz during the Swing Era—his prose had style, rhythm, bite, wallop, pizzazz—wrote this, nostalgically, about Goodman and the Swing Era in a 1961 *Boston Herald* column: "He haunted a whole generation and, for that matter, will continue to haunt it until its last member is in the ground, conjuring up, on phonograph records, more memory and more desire than any generation should ever have to bear." And if not every member of that generation, surely most who loved music.

Dan Morgenstern, director of the Institute of Jazz Studies, was too young (and in Europe) to remember the Swing Era, but he had it

24

Long Line in the Rain—Rain doesn't stop swing fans from lining up in hopes of getting a seat to see Benny Goodman's band at the Paramount Theater in New York City in 1940. (Copyright Frank Driggs Collection.)

right when he said that this period "must be recognized as the golden age of jazz." Decades ago there were jazz history books that suggested "real jazz" ended with Johnny Dodds, King Oliver, and Jelly Roll Morton in the 1920s, and some later writers have blithely and ignorantly assured readers there was no "real jazz" until the bop revolution, created largely by Charlie Parker and Dizzy Gillespie in the mid-1940s. So it's easy to understand why young students of jazz history are confused. One of the so-called "standard" jazz histories, a book translated into a dozen languages, is distressingly typical of many because it presents jazz before bop as being, if not somewhat inconsequential, mainly a prelude for much more important things to come. Thus in this too-oft-praised history, there are twenty-one references to Gillespie, eighteen to Parker, but only one to Benny Carter and none to Johnny Hodges or Art Tatum, although Carter, Hodges, and Tatum without question rank among the greatest jazz musicians of all time. And Goodman is not presented as an important jazz clarinetist, only as a bandleader. The Goodman trio, quartet, and sextet, all understandably highly praised by musicians and jazz fans alike, are not even mentioned. What kind of jazz history is this? Unbelievably, some other jazz history books are even worse.

But no matter what such books may contend, the Swing Era—not an earlier period, not a later period—was the golden age of jazz, and for many reasons. This was when good jazz musicians could find work, in big bands or in much smaller groups. This was when jazz had a large audience, when a good many jazz musicians were famous, and when audiences "would even applaud a good figuration," as Teddy Wilson said. This was when there were dozens of fine musicians on every instrument and when jazz soloists were delightfully individual.

It cannot be stressed too much: the Swing Era was when soloists did not sound like one another, when their approach to jazz improvisation was dissimilar. Who could possibly confuse Goodman with other standout clarinetists such as Artie Shaw, Fazola (aka Irving Prestopnik), Edmond Hall, or Pee Wee Russell? Or Goodman pianists Jess Stacy and Teddy Wilson? And Art Tatum, to be sure, played only and always like Art Tatum as he was the only one in the world who could.

Louis Armstrong influenced, directly or indirectly, all the major Swing Era trumpet soloists, but they found their own way of playing jazz on the trumpet. Who could confuse Roy Eldridge with Buck Clayton? Or Cootie Williams with Muggsy Spanier or Bunny Berigan or Charlie Shavers or Billy Butterfield or Harry James? Not anyone with ears. All of these players were quite remarkable and all sounded different.

Bob Crosby star Eddie Miller may have been one part Bud Freeman—maybe more like a dash, not a part—but he was certainly three parts Eddie Miller. Ben Webster began as an imitator of Coleman Hawkins but became one-of-a-kind Ben Webster, who could squeeze every last drop of succulent juice out of any decent melody. Benny Carter always sounded unmistakably like Benny Carter. Johnny Hodges played Johnny Hodges, the essence of musical heart and soul. And surely no one else on earth played the alto saxophone as did chunky Pete Brown, who used his sax as a piercing, tooting trumpet.

Yes, Peanuts Hucko tried to play like Goodman and sometimes succeeded, and many tenor men certainly tried to play like Coleman Hawkins or Lester Young, but players of the Swing Era were far more dissimilar than similar. Still to come were the days when most every young trumpet player tried to play like exciting bop trailblazer Dizzy Gillespie, who had given up trying to play like Roy Eldridge because Dizzy simply couldn't compete with Roy at Roy's own game. This post–Swing Era period was also when most young alto saxophonists tried to play like the ingenious Charlie Parker. And still to come were the years when so many tenor saxophonists sought to duplicate John Coltrane's "sheets of sound."

The trouble with all such imitation, the trouble with the countless imitators of Gillespie, Parker, Coltrane, whomever, is not only that most of them did not have the requisite skills but that such players often sounded precisely as if imitation was what they were trying to do. It's as if they were cloned. Hear one, hear them all, and rest assured they are not the real thing. Imitation breeds insincerity. Or, as Teddy Wilson told me, "when you imitate another musician's way of playing and are too derivative, your phrases are not too clear, are just a shade vague, and they lack real conviction." The point here is that slavish imitation and adoration were not predominant during the Swing Era. The idea was to dig other players, yes, but to play jazz your own way. Which, indeed, was what Gillespie and Parker did when they created the bop style that so many younger players imitated. Trumpet ace Clark Terry, who began his professional career toward the end of the Swing Era, was saying something like this when he told some jazz students: "Imitate, assimilate, and innovate."

There was much originality in the work of the best Swing Era players. But they did not strive for originality as much as they strove to play well. They did not reject tradition. They accepted tradition and enriched tradition. Swing music made the beat flow more compellingly, with the two-beat feel of the 1920s giving way to an even, usually unaccented four beats to a measure. The guitar and bass fiddle had replaced the banjo and tuba in rhythm sections, and jazz solos were stressed more than ever before even though proper intonation and reading music well became most important as big swing bands moved in. Still, Swing Era players were deeply influenced by the music and the great jazz players of the late 1920s, including Armstrong, Hines, Hawkins, and Jimmie Noone. Swing Era players were not involved in reinventing the wheel of jazz. In one sense, swing music wasn't new at all because it had been developing in many ways, often in those places where musicians gathered after work to play their kind of music, for kicks, long before the general public was aware of it.

Ellington's Sensuous Sounds

Of all the swing bands, most musicians and jazz enthusiasts seemed to agree that the Basie band *swung* the most. With a remarkable rhythm section and superb soloists such as Lester Young and Buck Clayton, the original Basie band was decidedly a player's band, not the arranger's band it became decades later. Indeed, the first Basie band relied mainly on "head" or memorized arrangements often based on tried-and-true chord progressions (the twelve-measure blues, *I Got Rhythm,* and other changes familiar to all good players).

But the most fascinating band in many ways was surely the one led by Ellington. And this one, despite all of its great soloists, was an arranger's orchestra with a full, sensuous, inimitable sound. With Harry Carney's baritone saxophone as anchor, even the reed section was eminently distinctive, being of greater harmonic breadth than the common four-man reed section of two alto and two tenor saxophones. Some of Ellington's music was also certainly more harmonically complex than was the norm in popular music. (When I was first learning guitar, I recall being impressed by the descending ninth—not seventh!—chords in his famous 1933 song *Sophisticated Lady.*)

Unlike other orchestra leaders, Ellington seldom bothered to play popular songs of the day or previous days. And why should he have been so bothered? After all, he and Billy Strayhorn could and did write their own "standards." During the Swing Era, Ellington played his older songs, such as *Sophisticated Lady, Mood Indigo* (1930), *Solitude* (1934), and *In a Sentimental Mood* (1935), but he kept adding other most pleasing pieces such as the haunting *Prelude to a Kiss* (1938), *I Let a Song Go Out of My Heart* (1938), *Flamingo* (1940), *All Too Soon* (1940), *I Got It Bad (And That Ain't Good)* (1941), and by his son Mercer, *Moon Mist* (1942). Lovely ballads by Billy Strayhorn that sounded sensuously perfect for Ellington players, especially Johnny Hodges, included *Day Dream* (1940), *Chelsea Bridge* (1941), and *Passion Flower* (1941).

Reminiscing in Tempo (1935) may have been unexciting, too long, and—as John Hammond contended—arty and pretentious. But no one who loved music could question the greatness of such 1940 three-minute gems as *Bojangles, A Portrait of Bert Williams, Ko-Ko, Jack the Bear, Warm Valley, In a Mellotone,* and *Never No Lament* (which translated into a hit popular song when it became *Don't Get Around Much Any More*), among other Ellington Swing Era pieces, some noted elsewhere in this book.

The stability of the Ellington orchestra, in marked contrast to most all other so-called big bands where personnel changes were frequent, made it easier for Ellington to create such marvelous music with and for

Superlative Team—Nonpareil composers and arrangers Billy Stayhorn and Duke Ellington. Strayhorn joined Ellington in 1939 and made Ellington's great music even greater. (Courtesy of Capitol Records and Tom Scanlan.)

his players and his orchestra. He knew precisely what his players, some with him for many years, could do. And he wrote specific pieces to showcase specific musicians in his band. *Concerto for Cootie,* featuring trumpet great Cootie Williams, was one of these. Recorded in 1940, this became the popular *Do Nothing Till You Hear From Me* when lyrics were added. And *Boy Meets Horn* (1938) demonstrated cornetist Rex Stewart's licks and tricks with half-valve quarter tones and other almost notes.

There are a few devout Ellingtonians who do not agree, but most consider Ellington's Swing Era band easily his best. If it did not swing as much or as persistently as the Basie band and perhaps several others, it certainly did swing on occasion as anyone who has heard *Cottontail* or the earlier *Rockin' in Rhythm* should know. In any event, the appeal of the Ellington orchestra was surely not limited to whether it swung all the time or not. Ellington was always in his own exceptional field of jazz activity. As the Swing Era faded into the bop "revolution,"

29

or evolution as some believe, it might be remembered that the popularity and fashions of bop did not alter Ellington's music in any significant way, if indeed at all.

If Ellington's Swing Era band had a weakness—and perfection is not only elusive but often boring—it was the rhythm section. Drummer Sonny Greer, with Ellington from 1918 on, was not to be compared to Basie's Jo Jones and other top drummers of the period including Sid Catlett, Dave Tough, Cozy Cole, and Chick Webb. So some contend that Greer was nevertheless just right for Ellington and possibly so, although this contention is usually made by those who find reason to believe that Ellington could do no wrong. And Ellington's guitar player, former banjoist Freddie Guy, with Ellington since the early 1920s, was in no way a standout guitarist nor a rhythmic force as were Freddie Green with Basie, or Allan Reuss (and later Benny Heller and Mike Bryan) with Goodman. Ellington always had fine bass players, however, including Billy Taylor, and from 1939–1941 wisely featured the remarkable young Jimmy Blanton, who more than anyone else made the bass viol a major solo instrument in jazz. Blanton's death at age twenty-one was a great tragedy for jazz music.

Despite the superb soloists in the Ellington orchestra, it was the prolific composing and arranging ingenuity of Ellington, harmonically and melodically, that firmly and distinctively characterized the band's music. Unlike bands led by Goodman, Shaw, Armstrong, Berigan, James, Carter, and many others, the Ellington band did not rise or fall on the performance of any single player. In contrast, a Goodman band without Goodman featured on almost every single piece would have been hard to imagine and surely not as commercially or artistically successful. Much the same is true of bands led by Goodman rival Shaw, always the primary soloist in his bands. But Ellington was not the solo star of his orchestra. Though a better pianist than some seem to realize, Ellington was not one of the great jazz piano players and his band did not stand or fall on how he played but on what he wrote for his truly exceptional "instrument," his orchestra.

"Itty Bitty Poo" Sold Well

It would be a mistake to think that jazz combos and the best swing bands completely ruled the roost during the Swing Era. Not at all. Many people strongly preferred Glenn Miller's "pardon me boy is that the" *Chattanooga Choo Choo* to any Basie, Ellington, or Goodman record. Frank Sinatra, known as "Frankie Boy" to his many thousands of adoring female teenage fans, singing *This Love of Mine* "goes on and on," or the livelier *Oh, Look at Me Now* with perky Connie Haynes and the Pied Pipers, certainly helped to assure Tommy Dorsey's continued success as much as *Opus 1* or *Well, Git It!* among other Luncefordian swingers by arranger Sy Oliver. And the Ink Spots, a saccharine vocal group never to be confused with the musically hip Mills Brothers, were a smash hit at Harlem's Apollo Theater. Ink Spot Bill Kenny, whose piercingly high tenor had the ladies swooning when he sang *If I Didn't Care,* was surely better known and more widely admired in black neighborhoods than Basie's robust blues belter Jimmy Rushing or any singer ever with Ellington.

Andy Kirk's band became nationally known because of how it played a ballad, *Until the Real Thing Comes Along,* not because of how his band played jazz. Kirk's distinctive romantic ballad singer, Pha Terrell, complete with falsetto, surely was as important to that band's success as its standout jazz players Mary Lou Williams and Dick Wilson.

Helen O'Connell, Jimmy Dorsey's appealing blonde singer with a wide smile and a limited vocal range she somehow made sexually provocative on such record hits as "those cool and limpid" *Green Eyes* and the undeniably groovy *Tangerine,* was much more widely known to the white audience than either Billie Holiday or Ella Fitzgerald. And if Ella had not recorded *A-Tisket, A-Tasket* ("I lost my yellow basket") with Chick Webb's band in 1938, a novelty song that became a surprise big seller, the marvelous Miss Fitzgerald would probably have been largely unknown to the general public.

Movie cowboy singer Gene Autry sold many more records in one year than Jack Teagarden did in a dozen years. "Sweet music" bandleader Horace Heidt and "His Musical Knights" had a runaway number one record seller with a song that combined a trite singsongy melody and inane lyrics, *I Don't Want to Set the World on Fire* ("I just want to start a flame in your heart"). The extraordinary jazz records produced by Milt Gabler for his Commodore label were not even dimly involved in the big-sales ballgame. In fact the great Commodore records, featuring dozens of great players including Teagarden, Freeman, Russell, Stacy, Chu Berry, Eldridge, and Mel Powell in a variety of small groups, were not available at most record stores and many jazz fans, including me, had to buy them by mail. This was also often true of the many fine small band recordings on the Keynote,

Chick and Ella!—This March 1939 photo of New York's Paramount Theater indicates how singer Ella Fitzgerald, then twenty-one years old, had increased the drawing power of Chick Webb's fine Savoy Ballroom Band. (Copyright Frank Driggs Collection.)

Blue Note, Signature, and Philo labels. Keynote twelve-inch sides included marvelous jazz by a Basie small group starring Buck Clayton and Lester Young with the pianist-leader billed on the label as "Prince Charming" because he was under contract to another company. On Philo, for Norman Granz, who was to become a rich and prolific producer of jazz records and jazz concerts, Lester teamed up with Nat Cole for superb twelve-inch recordings of *Indiana* and *Body and Soul*. Meanwhile, Kay Kyser had a best-seller with the childish *Three Little Fishes* "in a itty bitty poo," enough to gag the ungaggable.

Hollywood Was Never Hip

Many big bands were featured in movies during the Swing Era, including those led by Jimmy Dorsey, Tommy Dorsey, Ellington, Goodman, Herman, Miller, Barnet, James, Krupa, Joe Venuti, and

Charlie Spivak. But their performances were frequently shortchanged into background music for dumb plot-forwarding conversations by the stars of what did not become movie classics. There were minutes of good jazz in the movies, by Ellington, Goodman, and Waller included, but Hollywood was never hip and it rarely presented jazz of any kind well.

Of all who sang regularly in the movies, one of the best was Martha Raye, who had obvious jazz feeling and impeccable rhythmic time, but she was always cast as a goofy comedienne and a kind of comic singer. Raye did not get to sing the fine ballads written for the movies by Harry Warren, Jimmy Van Heusen, or Jimmy McHugh. Those songs were customarily sung by mediocre singers such as smoky-voiced Alice Faye, sarong-clad Dorothy Lamour, or famous-legs dancer Betty Grable.

Those who want to find some Swing Era music in old movies to slip into their VCR slots will discover *Stormy Weather, Cabin in the Sky* (including Ellington, Ethel Waters, and Lena Horne), *Reveille With Beverly* (with Ellington's band doing Strayhorn's famous *Take the 'A' Train* featuring Ray Nance), *Stage Door Canteen,* and *New Orleans* of possible interest. Also: *Hollywood Hotel* (Goodman), *Second Chorus* (Shaw), *Orchestra Wives* (Miller), *The Fleet's In* (Jimmy Dorsey), *Ship Ahoy!* (Tommy Dorsey), *Springtime in the Rockies* (James), among others. But the fast-forward button will be needed. Typical of how Hollywood handled jazz is *A Song Is Born,* where fast-forwarding will be gainfully employed to skip the incredibly stupid music-professors-discovering-and-defining jazz "plot" and the persistent mugging of Danny Kaye in order to find a few minutes of Louis Armstrong's great trumpet playing or Goodman, Lionel Hampton, and Mel Powell having fun *Stealin' Apples.*

A 1943 Academy Award-winning short filmed by Gjon Mili, *Jammin' the Blues,* was one of the best presentations of jazz ever on the silver screen. Among the players is Lester Young, shortly before Young was inducted into the Army and when his playing was absolutely marvelous. But such excellent jazz was extremely rare in the movies. The industry, as those in Hollywood called the movie business, didn't give a hoot about jazz. Perhaps this is why Billie Holiday was cast as a maid, or why in *Murder at the Vanities,* a 1934 movie, a gangster machine-guns the entire Ellington band.

"Soundies," movies for juke boxes, never really caught on and soon disappeared, but there is good jazz to be found on some of these three-minute films from the early 1940s, notably by Ellington. Alas, these are all produced with instrumental and vocal lip-synching to a previously recorded soundtrack.

Swing band leaders liked the pay and the publicity that came from being in the movies but had a right to be cynical about Hollywood's understanding of jazz. The later boring and misleading movie biographies of Gene Krupa and Benny Goodman—with Sal Mineo, of all actors, playing Krupa, and nonactor Steve Allen playing Goodman—proved how valid their cynicism was. *The Glenn Miller Story,* in contrast, was certainly commercially successful, but those who knew Miller, especially those who worked for him, can tell you that Miller was no Jimmy Stewart.

And any remembrance of the Swing Era should point out that during this period, as before and after, jazz was mainly an urban music. Country music of some kind, ranging from railroad songs to bluegrass, all of it known to most city people as "hillbilly" music then, was cherished by those living in sparsely populated hills and valleys, and in many cities proud not to be called big. Hank Williams was not yet an icon, but Roy Acuff and Kentucky's Bill Monroe, "the father of bluegrass," meant something emotionally and artistically important to countless thousands for whom the names Armstrong, Ellington, Goodman, and Basie meant little or more often absolutely nothing.

And while rural whites, plus some urban white sophisticates fascinated by the unsophisticated, found joy in country music, not jazz, hundreds of thousands of blacks bought so-called "race records" by blues singers who were unencumbered by any fancy jazz pretensions.

The blues has always been a blood-and-bone part of jazz music, but the blues preceded jazz and has its own tradition. The most heralded of all blues singers from a jazz standpoint is no doubt Bessie Smith, "Empress of the Blues." But it should be remembered that Bessie recorded with members of Fletcher Henderson's orchestra, notably cornetists Armstrong and Joe Smith, and her repertoire was not limited to the blues. Despite her role in jazz (many jazz players, including Bix Beiderbecke, loved her singing), the blues tradition—represented by several famous unrelated Smiths (Bessie, Trixie, and Clara), Ma Rainey, Ida Cox, and Blind Lemon Jefferson during the 1920s and Robert Johnson during the 1930s—had a vigorous life of its own apart from jazz, and was its own special thing, compellingly honest, unpretentious music with a vast rural and urban black audience. During the Swing Era, while others bought records by popular singers such as Bing Crosby, this audience waited for new releases by men such as Sonny Boy Williamson, Big Bill Broonzy, Blind Boy Fuller, Tampa Red (Hudson Whittaker), Leadbelly (Huddie Ledbetter, not limited to the blues by any means, as his biggest hit *Goodnight, Irene* suggests) and women such as Memphis Minnie (Lizzie Douglas), Lil Green, and Georgia White. Lil Green's *Why Don't You Do Right?* inspired Peggy Lee to get her boss Goodman to have an arrangement of that piece made for his band so she could sing it, and when this happened, Peggy Lee suddenly became famous. One of Georgia White's hit records, *I'll Keep Sitting on It,* was typical of the frank sexual comment, overflowing with double entendre, often found in the blues but almost never in any song from Tin Pan Alley.

Using traditional three-line stanzas in iambic pentameter, blues singers sang, usually with wry humor, about bad times and good times, true love and what some called raw lust, no-good men and no-good women, evil and funny happenings, despair and hope ("the sun's gonna shine in my back door someday"). And these blues singers reached the hearts, minds, and memories of many who had never heard of Roy Eldridge or Art Tatum, who did not know Lester Young from Lester Lanin.

Just as jazz was beginning to receive attention from the masses and some upper-crust music lovers enamored of Bach, Stravinsky, and perhaps Cole Porter, what had been viewed as common Negro blues singing suddenly became extraordinary expressions of truth and beauty to a growing group of young white admirers of black "folk" music.

The blues was called "the devil's music" in some black households, and during the Swing Era another kind of black music, seemingly opposite in subject matter to the blues, but similarly rhythmic, also received considerable attention. This was gospel music, related to the spirituals of years before, and first presented with wallop and unbridled passion in black churches. Gospel singers Rosetta Tharpe and the Golden Gate Quartet were certainly popular during the Swing Era.

Teenager Dinah Washington sang *I Know How to Do It* ("I may be square, I may be a bum, but I know how to do it") and other blues convincingly with Lionel Hampton, but it was no surprise when it was discovered that her career, when she was Ruth Jones, began with gospel singing. She was only one of many who moved from sacred to secular music. The reverse was rarer although there is one famous example: pianist-composer Thomas A. Dorsey, "The Father of Gospel Music." Dorsey was once "Georgia Tom," leader of Ma Rainey's band, a prolific blues writer and co-composer as well as co-performer with Tampa Red of the bawdy and enormously popular *It's Tight Like That* in 1928. "Georgia Tom" lived only on recordings when Dorsey switched to the Lord's music in the early 1930s. He wrote about 1,000 gospel songs including *Precious Lord, Take My Hand,* sung by Mahalia Jackson at the funeral of Martin Luther King, Jr. in 1968.

Most Swing Era jazz players, black or white, were big city people, but they could come from almost anywhere, including country towns, thanks in large measure to radio and the phonograph. The names of Swing Era musicians who came from small-town America are legion, and any jazz enthusiast can name prominent players who have more than a touch of country in their manner and in their music. Also, as Louis Armstrong said: "Who says I don't play folk music? I'm a folk."

During the Swing Era, "Kay Kyser's Kollege of Musical Knowledge" was more popular than any jazz radio program, but jazz was not hard to find on the radio or elsewhere. Even in restaurants and bars where there was no live music, there was often a busy jukebox. These fancy-lighted record-playing machines had been invented by Homer Capehart in 1934, and within a year or so they seemed to be almost everywhere. It cost me five cents to hear, say, Bunny Berigan's glorious trumpet solo on Tommy Dorsey's *Marie,* a nickel well spent although hearing this record cost as much a double-scoop Breyer's ice cream cone or a freshly made soda fountain Coca-Cola.

Swing Sampler, Late 1941

As for live music, what follows is a mere sampling of what could be heard in different cities when the Swing Era was in full swing, specifically a month or so before the Japanese bombed Pearl Harbor on December 7, 1941, "a day that will live in infamy," President Roosevelt said, and a day that brought the United States into World War II.

Jimmie Lunceford's entertaining, distinctive, and smartly dressed band was two-beating with style and grace at the Strand Theater in Brooklyn. The superb Ellington band was working one-nighters on the West Coast.

(Earlier that year, Ellington's musical revue *Jump for Joy* ran for six weeks in a Los Angeles theater. In addition to Ellington's music and orchestra, it included comedians, dancers, singers, and beautiful women, notably Dorothy Dandridge. Dancer Marie Bryant did a hip and hip-vibrating *Chocolate Shake,* Joe Turner shouted the blues wallopingly, Ellington's star singer Ivie Anderson handled *Rocks in*

My Bed and the revue's show-stopper *I Got It Bad* [singing the original fine lyrics by Paul Webster, specifically a bridge that included "my man and me we gin some, embrace some, and sin some," seldom heard for many years now, having been altered by bluenose powers-that-be], and handsome Herb Jeffries sang such songs as *The Brownskin Gal in the Calico Gown* as well as the lively title song ["Fare thee well, land of cotton, cotton lisle is out of style, honey chile, jump for joy ..."]. Some said the show was ahead of its time. But recalling that several all-black revues had been smash hits on Broadway, there were New Yorkers who suggested that *Jump for Joy* was presented on the wrong coast of America for true theatrical success.)

At Hollywood's Cafe Society, Billie Holiday was snapping her fingers and kicking her right heel, pushing the beat, while swinging *What a Little Moonlight Can Do* or *Them There Eyes* for her old fans and enrapturing newer ones with stylized slow-to-slowest torch songs and the always reverentially greeted, hush-she's-going-to-sing-it *Strange Fruit,* a succinct commentary on the horror of lynching. "Southern trees bear a strange fruit ... ."

Also in L.A., at the Swanee Inn, Meade Lux Lewis, master of eight-beats-to-the-bar boogie-woogie, was demonstrating how to truly chug *Honky Tonk Train Blues.* Jimmy Dorsey, who had 3,400 people showing up for his weekday opening night at the Hollywood Palladium on Sunset Boulevard, had moved to the East, where he set a new box-office financial record for a single night at Frank Dailey's Meadowbrook on November 22. And on November 25, back at the Palladium, a new band led by Stan Kenton cracked an opening night record that had been held by—yes—Jimmy Dorsey. Admission to the Palladium was well under two dollars a couple and dinner was about $1.75.

Premier jazz violinist and delightful storyteller Joe Venuti, an irrepressible swinger and a major jazz player by the mid-1920s, was at the Paramount Theater in Toledo. Louis Jordan's amusing Tympany Five could be heard at the 113 Club in Grand Forks, North Dakota, and the alto saxophonist was surely singing his 1941 hits *I'm Gonna Move to the Outskirts of Town* (that's mo-oo-oo-oove, as he sang it) and *Knock Me a Kiss* (yet to come was *Five Guys Named Moe*).

Raymond Scott, known for a quintet that played unusual quasi-jazz originals such as *Huckleberry Duck* and *Twilight in Turkey* and for writing the lament *When Cootie Left the Duke* had a big band at the Brunswick Hotel in Boston. Cab Calloway was hi-de-hi-de-hi-de-hoing and prancing around with his hair swirling into his face while

Where Thousands Danced—One of the most famous ballrooms on the West Coast, the Hollywood Palladium on Sunset Boulevard showcased the great big bands. (Copyright Frank Driggs Collection.)

leading an orchestra of exceptional jazz players at the New Kenmore Hotel in Albany. Cab, and the world of jazz, had lost his great tenor sax player, Chu Berry, thirty-one years old, in an October 30 auto crash on an Ohio country road.

Bunny Berigan, who would die at age thirty-three in June 1942 (they said the cause of death was pneumonia but his many friends suspected alcohol may have had something to do with it), had left Tommy Dorsey again and was leading his last band. In Wilkes-Barre, Pennsylvania, Berigan played to a crowd of 1,500 people in Berwick Park.

Pianist Jay McShann's band, with Charlie Parker in the reed section, was playing in the Blue Room of the Streets Hotel in Kansas City after completing a two-month road trip on the "Gopher-Meadowland" circuit of Texas, Missouri, and Oklahoma. In St. Louis, they danced to the bands of Dipsy-Doodler Larry Clinton, who would pilot an Army Air Corps plane the next year, and Jack Teagarden in the Casa Loma Ballroom. Meanwhile, Glen Gray's Casa Loma band, named for a hotel in Toronto where this orchestra got started way back in 1928, was playing *Smoke Rings* at the Totem Pole in Newton's Norembega Park, near Boston.

Charlie Spivak, known for his fine trumpet tone, had a string of one-nighters in the Midwest and one of his three trombonists was the then unknown Nelson Riddle. Pianist Bob Zurke, one of the top Bob Cats in Bob Crosby's band, followed another famous and even greater Bob Cat pianist, hefty Joe Sullivan, at Mitch's Tavern in Mendota, Minnesota, near Minneapolis.

Andy Kirk and "His Clouds of Joy," without tenor sax star Dick Wilson who died in late November, had completed a week at the Apollo Theater in Harlem and was back where he so often was, "on wheels" as he called it, before reaching the Tune Town Ballroom in St. Louis where he was on December 7, that day of infamy. Also on the road was the band led by the great pianist Earl Hines, and one of his typical gigs was in Uniontown, Pennsylvania. Tenor saxophonist Budd Johnson was a star soloist and also with "Fatha" Hines at this time was handsome Billy Eckstine, who no doubt caught the ears and eyes of many young ladies and sang *Jelly, Jelly* every night.

Another good bet: on the road with Lionel Hampton's popular band, nineteen-year-old Illinois Jacquet had them yelling "go, go, go!" every night as he built chorus-after-chorus of full-throated, rip-roaring, rhythmic excitement on *Flying Home*. Though his most famous tenor sax solo habitually moved into honks, groans, and screeching high notes, it began as a compelling melodic improvisation, which is why so many, including this writer, knew by heart the opening chorus of his solo as recorded in 1942. We also knew Ben Webster's tenor solo on Ellington's 1940 *Cottontail* by heart, and some of us could hum, mumble, whistle, scat sing, or think Lester Young solos for the same melodic reason.

Artie Shaw, whose upper register on the clarinet was beyond compare, had one of his best bands, one that earned rare pay of $10,000 for theater dates. Shaw was on the road a month before Pearl Harbor, playing in Oklahoma City, Omaha, elsewhere in the Midwest, and Philadelphia. Big bands got around without using airplanes.

Also in Philly at that time, local clarinetist Billy Krechmer was holding sessions at his small "Jam Session" club on narrow Ransted Street, where Leopold Stokowski sometimes listened and which was only steps away from a tailor shop run by Reggie Jackson's father. And the King Cole Trio was at Philadelphia's 20th Century Club. Nat was best known as a pianist, but, hey, he could really sing, too!

In Chicago, Jimmie Noone, a great clarinetist who moved to the Windy City from New Orleans in 1918 and was praised by Goodman and anyone else who knew anything about jazz clarinet, led a combo at the "Yes, Yes" club, while nonpareil Louis Armstrong was at the Grand Terrace Cafe fronting a big band that did not bat in his league. Years before there was a Swing Era, the Grand Terrace, on the South Side's East Thirty-fifth Street, was the home of the Earl Hines Orchestra, heard regularly on network radio, and one place in the city that welcomed both black and white patrons.

Fats Waller was doing four and sometimes five shows daily at the South Side's famous Regal Theater, breaking everyone up and no doubt drinking shots "three fingers neat" backstage. Veteran Eddie South, billed as "The Dark Angel of the Violin," a masterful player whose music was not always jazz but always good, was at the Capitol Lounge. Coleman Hawkins, known as "Bean" or "The Hawk" to his many admirers, was creating new melodies, not just running chord changes as few ever could, with a combo at Dave's Swingland. Les Brown's musically hip band, featuring fine clarinet by Abe Most, was pleasing dancers, as usual, at the Blackhawk, and Will Bradley's band had bused from theater dates in Akron and Youngstown to the popular Panther Room at the Hotel Sherman.

In Kelly's Stables on Fifty-second Street in New York, a seven-piece band led by Benny Carter, with Dizzy Gillespie on trumpet and Jimmy Hamilton on clarinet, shared the bandstand with Art Tatum, properly described by pianist-writer Don Asher as "the Father, Son, and Holy Ghost to jazz pianists." Elsewhere on The Street, veteran New Orleans and Chicago drummer Zutty Singleton led a group of traditional jazzmen at Jimmy Ryan's, and clarinetist Joe Marsala, who may have made more money from his ballad *Don't Cry, Joe* ("let her go, let her go, let her go") than he did playing first-class jazz, was back at his old stomping ground, the Hickory House. Accomplished drummer George Wettling was with him, assuring a solid beat. The Hickory House, so named because it served steaks broiled over hickory logs, was larger and quite different from other Fifty-second Street clubs, with an oval bandstand, not at the rear of the room, but behind a bar surrounded by tables.

Herschel Evans was dead and Lester Young was no longer with the Count Basie band, but at Cafe Society Uptown, the Count still had two fine tenor sax soloists, Don Byas and Buddy Tate. Byas demonstrated how smooth, warm, and polished improvisations could be, and Texan Tate bubbled over with rambunctious, booting, hell-for-leather solo attacks of irresistible rhythmic power. Stylish trumpet players Buck Clayton and Harry (Sweets) Edison were still with Basie, as was his matchless rhythm trio of guitarist Freddie Green, big and big-toned bass player Walter Page (appropriately called "Big 'Un" by Basie), and drummer Jo Jones, who "played like the wind," they said, accurately. Also, to the pleasure of all, Basie at this time was not at all reluctant about taking piano solos.

At Cafe Society Downtown, on Sheridan Square in Greenwich Village, you could hear Teddy Wilson, boogie-woogie pianist Albert Ammons, and singer Lena Horne, replaced by Helen Humes when the lovely Lena departed, reportedly for Hollywood. In this club, opened in 1938 as one of the first in New York outside of Harlem to encourage an integrated audience as well as white and black on the bandstand, a good dinner was available for under two bucks.

One of Goodman's best bands was in the midst of a five-month engagement at the Hotel New Yorker's Terrace Room. This band featured ingenious pieces by Eddie Sauter (for example, *Benny Rides Again* and *Clarinet à la King*), the Teagardenesque trombone of Lou McGarity, the commanding lead horn of big Jimmy Maxwell, and sitting beside him in the trumpet section, one of the Swing Era's great players, short and chubby Billy Butterfield, affectionately called "Butterball." There were two teenagers: eighteen-year-old pianist Mel Powell, and an attractive nineteen-year-old blonde from North Dakota who had changed her name from Norma Egstrom to Peggy Lee. She was somewhat unsure of herself at the microphone, did not articulate words clearly as earlier BG singers Mildred Bailey and Helen Forrest did, had been panned by jazz critics (John Hammond told Goodman that Miss Lee simply could not sing), and was only beginning to learn her trade, which she eventually transformed into artistry. Cootie Williams had just left Goodman to begin his own band, and Benny's ace electric guitarist with the sextet, Charlie Christian, was missing. Christian was still on salary but hospitalized in the Seaview Sanitarium on Staten Island where he would die in March 1942 at age twenty-five.

Harry James was playing his new hit version of the old tune *You Made Me Love You* at the Hotel Lincoln but remembered to swing a few, too. And Glenn Miller's most popular orchestra was drawing big crowds to the Cafe Rouge of the Hotel Pennsylvania, a much larger room than the basement Madhattan Room at that hotel where Goodman had them jumping in 1938. The Glenn Miller theme, *Moonlight Serenade,* and other Miller pieces, with the clarinet "on top" playing lead melody over the saxophones, was a lovely, appealing, and dreamy romantic sound, many insisted. Good dance music, too. The Miller band was not the swingingest band around and was as commercial in its way as many bands that did not begin to compare with it musically, but thousands, maybe millions, thought that dancing to the smooth Miller music was almost like being in love. And this was certainly a well-rehearsed band. Also, let's add that in music, as in other artistic endeavors, there has always been good commercial as well as bad commercial. Miller's popular music was good commercial and sometimes excellent commercial. Miller did not tolerate sloppy playing.

Elsewhere in New York, at Nick's, located at Seventh Avenue and Tenth Street in Greenwich Village, the driving cornet of slick-haired Wild Bill Davison was leading a group of Eddie Condon buddies in a no-nonsense, straightforward, roof-raising demonstration of what many believed to be the truth, the whole truth, and nothing but the truth. Perish the thought that written music of any kind could ever be needed here. And some who played at Nick's, including Davison, could not have read music anyway. This was also the place where Eddie Condon called the men's room attendant Flush Gordon. (Though known for its excellent Dixieland or "Nicksieland" music, the King Cole Trio, not yet famous and certainly not in any kind of Dixieland groove, had recently worked an intermission gig at Nick's, with Nat making forty-five dollars a week and his two sidemen thirty dollars. A few years later Nat's weekly income was MUCH higher—and properly so.)

Across the George Washington Bridge in Englewood, New Jersey, Teddy Powell had been leading a good big band at the Rustic Cabin, but early one morning the club burned down and his instruments and arrangements were destroyed. Luckily, Powell had copies of most of these valuable charts and was back at work in the Plymouth Theater in Worcester, Massachusetts, shortly before the bombing of Pearl Harbor.

A fine trumpet player, Frankie Newton, led a ten-piece band including Vic Dickenson on trombone at the Mimo, a Harlem club partly owned by tap dancer Bill Robinson, the famous "Bojangles." Red Norvo was rehearsing a new band, with Alec Wilder writing many of his arrangements, and getting set to open at the Blue Gardens in Armonk, New York. Bob Chester's underrated band was at the Log Cabin also in this town north of White Plains.

At the Glen Island Casino in New Rochelle, New York (a town described in song by George M. Cohan years before as *Only Forty-Five Minutes From Broadway* after he moved there), Claude Thornhill was delighting dancers and the musically aware with some harmonically fascinating work by new arranger Gil Evans. Beside Glen Island Casino, close to the small Army island of Fort Slocum, youngsters in rowboats could hear good music free.

Hal McIntyre, who had been Glenn Miller's crack lead alto player for five years, had a new band on tour in New England and was signed for a Glen Island Casino engagement to run from January until May. (The next summer, between sets at the Million Dollar Pier in Atlantic City, McIntyre said that "the one thing" he "really missed" about the Miller band was listening to Bobby Hackett play "during the dinner hour." This was apparently about the only time Miller featured the

Moonlight Serenade Heard Here—The Glen Island Casino on Long Island Sound in New Rochelle, New York, near the Army's Fort Slocum, a small island post. Many bands became popular here, including one organized in 1938 by trombonist-arranger Glenn Miller. Small boats anchored around the club when bands were playing. (Copyright Frank Driggs Collection.)

43

great cornet player. Unfortunately this work Hackett did with Miller was never recorded. Hackett was heard briefly on a few Miller records, but the major soloist on most Miller records was saxophonist Tex Beneke, most certainly not in Hackett's league.)

Ella Fitzgerald was on a theater tour, fronting the band once led by gallant drummer Chick Webb, who had died in 1939. Also working the black theater circuit were bands led by Les Hite, with whom Lionel Hampton played before joining Goodman, and Don Redman, one of jazz music's earliest and greatest big band arrangers, who wrote for Henderson and McKinney's Cotton Pickers during the 1920s. Woody Herman's "Band That Plays the Blues," with female trumpet player Billie Rogers, drew a crowd of 4,000 for a University of Minnesota ball in Minneapolis.

And all of this big and small band activity, shortly before Pearl Harbor, was merely a small slice of what was happening in jazz then. Hundreds of other bands—good and not-so-good—were working in clubs, ballrooms, and hotels. Jam sessions also were not uncommon.

Gone With the Draft

After Pearl Harbor, big bands lost more key players to the Army, the King Cole Trio's *Gone With the Draft* became more meaningful to musicians, and Hot Lips Page sang a blues he called *Uncle Sam Ain't No Woman but He Certainly Can Steal Your Man*. Some band leaders simply gave up. *Metronome*'s George Simon quoted Will Bradley explaining it this way in 1942: "We were playing in Detroit when they took six men from us all at one time—most of them trumpets. From there we had to go directly to Denver. Now, where could you find six men in Denver to replace the guys we'd lost? I had no idea, so I didn't even try. I just gave up the band."

Artie Shaw was soon a chief petty officer leading a Navy orchestra in the Pacific. His players included Claude Thornhill, trumpet ace Max Kaminsky, and superb drummer Dave Tough. And Glenn Miller was a captain, then major, leading a large, versatile Army Air Forces orchestra in England that included Mel Powell, who led the orchestra's small jazz combo, and other big band standouts such as drummer Ray McKinley, clarinetist Peanuts Hucko, and guitarist Carmen Mastren. Johnny Mince, the excellent clarinet soloist with Tommy Dorsey, was an Army private playing in the pit band of Irving Berlin's all-soldier show *This Is the Army*. Star drummer Buddy Rich was a

Wartime Player—Clarinetist great Artie Shaw shown here as a U.S. Navy Chief Petty Officer, in the November 1, 1943, issue of Down Beat. *(Reprinted with permission from* Down Beat *magazine.)*

Marine, and another top young drummer, Shelly Manne, was in the Coast Guard. Willie Smith, the superlative lead alto player of Lunceford's marvelous reed section, was in a Navy band at the Great Lakes training center.

Many other prominent players were drafted, including Buck Clayton, Jo Jones, Bud Freeman, and Joe Bushkin. Others enlisted to join specific service bands. In March 1943, Jack Teagarden said he had lost seventeen men to the Army or Navy in four months. This was understandable. There was a war going on. And many young men who were drafted did react with bewilderment and sometimes anger to the news that bobby-soxer favorite Frank Sinatra was ruled an undraftable 4-F because he reportedly had, of all things, a punctured eardrum. This was another reminder that draft boards differed from state to state, and just who was drafted was based partly on how many men were needed from different states at different times. As always, all was not fair in love or war.

Admission of marijuana use and racial prejudice led unlikely soldier Lester Young to Army imprisonment—thus his later piece *D.B. Blues,* the initials standing for Disciplinary Barracks—and his fifteen months in Uncle Sam's Army were decidedly not happy ones. Because of age or medical reasons, many other famous players remained civilians. Ellington was not involved, being over forty in 1941, and Basie was thirty-seven that year, Hines thirty-six. By 1942, the government said no one over thirty-eight would be drafted. Goodman, thirty-two in 1941, was 4-F because of severe sciatica and a slipped disc that led to surgery at the Mayo Clinic in 1940, an operation that was not fully successful. His back problem bothered him for the rest of his life and explained why he sometimes leaned against the piano during a solo and often preferred to sit on a stool while playing music in later years. His condition did, however, give him a title for one of his sextet hits: *Slipped Disc.*

During the war there was much excellent jazz produced free by musicians on V-discs ("V" for victory) for servicemen and broadcast by the Armed Forces Radio Service. This writer still cherishes those I shipped home from Okinawa after these thin, twelve-inch, shatterproof records were about to be tossed away as our tiny Army radio station folded. The theme for a jazz program I had on this station in 1945 was taken from one of these V-discs and indicated how rare some V-disc jazz was: a blues that began with an Art Tatum piano introduction to a Louis Armstrong trumpet solo! (This came from a January 1944 *Esquire* all-star jazz concert at New York's Metropolitan Opera House. V-discs were not subject to the recording ban in force at that time.)

The Swing Era continued during World War II years after Pearl Harbor but in somewhat diminished capacity. There were fewer good big bands on the road, and by 1946 many younger musicians were enraptured with Charlie Parker and the revolutionary jazz called bebop. On the big band scene, Woody Herman's great "First Herd" swung hard from 1943–1946. It was infinitely superior to Herman's earlier band, the one that produced the popular *Woodchopper's Ball,* an up-tempo blues. Herman's "First Herd" was Woody's *Apple Honey* band that had exciting arrangements by Ralph Burns and Neal Hefti. It featured solos by Brooklyn tenor saxophonist Joe "Flip" Phillips and inimitable Philadelphia trombonist Bill Harris, whose instrument was a fiery furnace of thunder, lightning, and continual surprise. But small band jazz seemed to dominate during the war. Big bands had trouble finding capable players, and the 1942 recording ban imposed by musicians union chief James C. Petrillo continued until 1944. The ban hurt big bands and resulted only in a union-controlled fund into which record companies paid a fee for each record made. The ban did help singers, however, making some of them household names as they produced jukebox hits while bands were grounded from recording studios.

One-nighters became fewer as gas rationing and restrictions on buying new tires made it tough for bands to use buses or autos.

Chartering private railroad coaches or Pullmans ended because movement of men in uniform was more important. Musicians who grumbled about such problems were asked, reasonably, "don't you know there's a war on?" And some out-of-town ballrooms closed simply because patrons couldn't get the gas needed to drive to them. (Most people, with an "A" card, were allowed only three gallons of gas a week.) It was the beginning of the end for many big bands. Detroit concentrated on Army jeeps, not new cars, and even musical instrument manufacturers were converted to producing war equipment. Some piano makers made gliders instead.

Before duty overseas, during Army furloughs I discovered there was still music on Fifty-second Street, including Art Tatum, Billie Holiday, and Coleman Hawkins, all of whom I also heard in small Washington clubs during the war years. And I did talk to soft-spoken modest Fletcher Henderson in Great Bend, Kansas, of all places, as he rehearsed his last band, one that seemed as tired as he obviously was that day. Being on the road was still possible but certainly not much fun. His band struggled with the famous Henderson and Don Redman charts, and his band bus looked as if it must have struggled, too.

By 1946, when I was a civilian again, Eddie Condon had opened his club in Greenwich Village, where the four-string guitarist moved from table to table dispensing examples of his famed wit and where the music was always lively, if not as innovative as some jazz critics wished. James P. Johnson was sometimes intermission pianist. I wondered then how many at the club knew who this unpretentious, older big black man with the cigar in his mouth, called Jimmy by Condon, was. (Johnson helped to move ragtime into jazz. He was one of Harlem's first and greatest stride pianists, and he influenced Fats Waller enormously. Johnson also wrote such successful songs as *If I Could Be With You, Charleston, Runnin' Wild,* and his earlier piano piece *Carolina Shout* was learned by heart from piano rolls by Ellington and many other young jazz pianists in the early 1920s. Any history of jazz piano is incomplete without appropriate attention paid to Johnson.) And there were also Sunday afternoon jam sessions in New York, notably at Jimmy Ryan's on Fifty-second Street, where such masters as Sidney Bechet, J. C. Higginbotham, and Lips Page sat in and where the entrance fee to attend one of these all-star sessions was only one buck.

As is well known, forty-year-old Major Glenn Miller was aboard an Air Force plane that took off from England to France in mid-December

1944, and that plane was never seen again. As is not well known, also lost to music because of the war was Otis Ferguson, the writer. A sailor as a teenager, at age thirty-five he was not about to be drafted but wanted to serve somehow and signed up with the Merchant Marine. While his ship was anchored in the Gulf of Salerno, a radio-guided bomb released from a German plane hit the messroom where Ferguson was having a cup of coffee. He was the only one aboard who was killed.

After the war, big band musicians arrived home to discover jobs were scarce. In one month, December 1946, bands led by Woody Herman, Benny Goodman, Tommy Dorsey, Harry James, Les Brown, Jack Teagarden, and Benny Carter all disbanded. Some returned, including Herman a year later with his *Four Brothers* "Second Herd," but the big band business would never be the same. Singers were suddenly more popular than big bands, and by the end of the 1940s bop dominated the psyches of most young jazz musicians (Ruby Braff was a notable exception to this generality). Enormously gifted and highly original, Charlie Parker became a kind of modern jazz god despite his heroin addiction and heavy drugs infiltrating the jazz scene as never before. Swing music had been a continuation of the jazz tradition that preceded it, but bop was revolutionary. And no matter how challenging and thrilling some of bop's harmonic innovations may have been, no matter how many jazz critics were mesmerized by it, bop was not for dancers. Nor, some insisted, for melody lovers. Ballrooms closed and jazz clubs became harder to find.

During the Swing Era, most of the big bands had female singers. Some were hired because they looked good although they sometimes sang out of tune or out of time. Demonstrating the same kind of "sex sells" show-biz habit, two nonsingers, Ina Ray Hutton, former Ziegfeld showgirl, and the not as famous stunning brunette Ada Leonard, former stripper, became bandleaders and not because they knew anything about music. For Hutton, a popular baton-waving mover and shaker, a specialty was wearing a variety of gee-whiz tight gowns, sometimes changed between sets.

But some young women became big band singers because they could really sing. These included Mildred Bailey, Helen Forrest, Ella Fitzgerald, Mary Ann McCall, Rosemary Clooney, and Helen Humes. Others combined distinctive beauty and true singing ability and two sterling examples were Helen Ward and Doris Day. Some big bands had male singers, too, and among the best were Dick Haymes, Frank Sinatra, Perry Como, and Bob Eberly. Bob sang with Jimmy Dorsey. His brother Ray (with last name spelled Eberle) was equally well known because he sang with Glenn Miller. And both brothers were certainly much better known to the general public than many important jazz players, including two of Duke Ellington's personal heroes: remarkable soprano saxophonist Sidney Bechet (he could not read music and who cared?) and the dapper, loquacious William Henry Joseph Bonaparte Bertholoff Smith, one of the Harlem piano kings and a prolific composer known to all as The Lion, Willie "The Lion" Smith.

Still, despite the fame of many band singers during the Swing Era, and except for Bing Crosby and a few others, the Swing Era was when musicians, not singers, made the money. Sinatra, with Harry James and Tommy Dorsey, and Helen Forrest, with Artie Shaw and Benny Goodman, were paid less than $100 a week while musicians in those bands were making $150 to $300 and a few key sidemen considerably more. Forrest, one of the best big band singers, certainly made more than $100 per week with the Harry James band, but she was featured as never before, singing more than the customary one chorus per tune. Her joyful, rhythmically certain, lilting voice was a major reason for many of the best-selling records by James, including *You Made Me Love You* and *I've Heard That Song Before,* both of which sold over one million copies. After the Swing Era, many former big band singers—Sinatra, Haymes, Como, Doris Day (who became a movie star), Rosemary Clooney, Patti Page, Peggy Lee, Kay Starr, Jo Stafford, Sarah Vaughan, Dinah Washington, to list only some—were making more money than almost all of the musicians they had worked with and for.

By the late 1950s, the Swing Era was long gone and jazz had serious problems as youngsters discovered their own kind of popular music that was certainly not any kind of jazz. This was rock 'n' roll. It was produced, jazz people contended, by obvious amateurs. Charlie Barnet spoke for the Swing Era generation when he called rock "an insult to the world of music," adding that "much of it seems to be performed by mental cases and untalented misfits … . I couldn't believe what was happening, the inmates had taken over the asylum."

But whether produced by untalented misfits or not, loudly amplified and unsophisticated rock was for millions of kids an easy, clean knockout winner over jazz, and jazz never ever recovered the popularity it had during the Swing Era. Also an eventual winner was rhythm and blues, black parent of rock, music that was seldom what jazz musicians, white or black, meant by the words "rhythm" and "blues."

A few big bands hung on for many years after the Swing Era, including exceptional ones led by Ellington, Herman, and Basie. And Swing Era stars kept playing their kind of great music in small bands, usually, to a smaller group of devoted fans as many prominent jazz critics all but ignored them as they enthused over bop, hard bop, and "new thing" players. What jazz would be "tomorrow" curiously became important to some who persistently viewed jazz as a problem to be solved, not as music to enjoy.

A good many jazz fans became former jazz fans as they wondered where all the melody had gone. They were told, but were not convinced, that melody is only whatever the improvising jazz player plays. Swing Era types also noted with disdain the loss of dynamics in much of the newer jazz music. The loud and soft of it all, the fortissimo and pianissimo, the smashing crackle of a brass section followed by the much softer sounds of unamplified rhythm instruments behind a piano solo, as exemplified by the Basie band, seemed to be all but lost as hard boppers and other young jazz musicians continuously kept their music at the same unwavering loud volume level.

For some of us, the Swing Era was over all too soon. Jazz concerts with people sitting in rows staring at the musicians replaced the camaraderie that went along with jazz in the clubs. Similar row-sitting in auditoriums listening to the remaining decent big bands replaced dancing in ballrooms. As one who had danced to Ellington, Basie, Goodman, Shaw, Barnet, Herman, and many others, I never felt I could somehow hear and appreciate big band music better sitting in a chair, but some jazz-must-be-art-and-not-dance-music critics had the idea that jazz concerts raised the artistic appreciation level for jazz. Or something. Maybe they simply could not or did not like to dance.

By the late 1940s, the Swing Era was all but dead. What was once known as swing alley, specifically those brownstone ground floor nightclubs between Fifth and Sixth Avenues on West Fifty-second in Manhattan, had become strip row. Female flesh had replaced jazz music. On the bandstand at the Three Deuces where Coleman Hawkins, Big Sid Catlett, Lester Young, and other jazz giants swung during the Swing Era, someone billed as Zorita danced with a live snake. At the Famous Door, where Count Basie created great swing excitement in 1938, where Billie Holiday sent chills up and down the spine, customers drank overpriced and overwatered whiskey as they joined

B-girls and pimps to oggle someone named Titza perform a "wine dance." Hoodlums and drug peddlers now dominated The Street, not musicians. And it wasn't long before the wrecker's steel ball and bulldozers arrived, followed by more tall buildings for midtown Manhattan.

The death of The Street in the 1940s was a symbolic end to the Swing Era, a time when jazz was melodic and popular, when jazz meant dancing, fun, and joy, when jazz was not a subject for college study like, say, old Italian movies.

Benny Goodman Quartet—The famous Benny Goodman Quartet in 1938, just after Dave Tough had replaced Gene Krupa on drums. The other three: Lionel Hampton on vibes, Goodman on clarinet, and Teddy Wilson on piano. (Copyright Frank Driggs Collection.)

2

White, Black, Brown, and Beige

"I played with Pearl Bailey once [in Las Vegas] when both of us had to stay in our dressing rooms because no hotel wanted anything that looked like us."

—Benny Payne

 Racial Problems, inspired by racial prejudices and hatreds, have bedeviled America from the beginning. And during the Swing Era, Jim Crow played a major, demeaning role.

Working in a black band was enormously different from working in a white band. The pay was almost always lower, "the road" was often a humiliating, gut-wrenching place to make a living, and it could be perilous to your health as well. Covert racism was present as well as the blatant, in-your-face, officially sanctioned kind. Problems extended beyond "whites only" restrictions involving hotels, rooming houses, restaurants, drinking fountains, and toilets.

The Ellington band often lived on the train when on tour, and for good reason, especially but not only in the South. Ellington's movable hotel consisted of two Pullman cars plus baggage car, before World War II made such an escape from segregation realities impossible. The Cab Calloway band also traveled in its own Pullman for some time and Cab was somehow able to transport his big green Lincoln convertible in the band's baggage car.

Many black bands (not the two most financially successful ones, led by Ellington and Calloway) had to spend eight months on the road each year because location jobs simply were not as available to black bands as to white bands. Many hotels and ballrooms would not hire black bands. And just where a black band on tour could stay was always a problem. Andy Kirk recalled a New York company called Travelguide: "I told Travelguide about all the little black hotels and homes where we stayed, and that way blacks traveling in different parts of the country had a reference book to guide them out of embarrassing situations."

Andy Razaf (born Andreamentania Paul Razafkeriefo, son of a nephew of the queen of Madagascar) summed up this sad situation with lyrics for a 1929 Fats Waller show tune, *Black and Blue*. The song asks a proper question: "My only sin is in my skin. What did I do to be so black and blue?"

Words of similar, if slyer, import could be heard almost twenty years earlier in 1910 lyrics written by Cecil Mack (aka Richard McPherson) to a lively melody by Ford Dabney: *(That's Why They Call Me) Shine*. During the Swing Era, this was a popular standard, played by the Goodman Sextet and many other prominent groups, often sung too, but has seldom been heard since. It concludes: "Just because my color's shady, that makes a little difference, *maybe,* that's why they call me shine."

Cab Calloway remembered that in 1932 "in some places like Winston-Salem and Atlanta they had a rope down the middle of the dance hall with the Negroes dancing on one side and the whites on the other." There was segregation in the North, too. When the Basie band played its first engagement in New York in 1936, at the famous Roseland Ballroom where hostesses at that time earned only ten cents a dance, blacks were not permitted in. And John Hammond, ardent promoter of the Basie band and an equally ardent proponent of desegregation *everywhere,* recalled this about Basie's famous steady summer gig at the Famous Door on Fifty-second Street in 1938: "Tempting as the Famous Door engagement was, there was a major problem. The place had no air conditioning, and I knew Basie couldn't make it through the summer without it. I put up the money for the cooling system on the condition the club allow Negro patronage, which was virtually unheard of in midtown New York then. The owners reluctantly agreed. The band came in and jammed the place nightly when word got around."

Willard Alexander, booking agent for Basie, as well as others including Goodman, remembered this quite differently, saying that MCA, the booking agency, put up the money. In any event, segregation on The Street ended. But it remained firm in many places, North, East, West, and South, during the Swing Era.

As for Hollywood, Lena Horne recalled this about her 1942 movie debut in *Panama Hattie:* "I did a musical number that was not integrated into the script. The idea was that it could be cut out of the film, without spoiling it, by local distributors if they thought their audiences would object to seeing a Negro. It was ridiculous, but that's how show business—and especially the movies—docilely bowed to prejudice." Yes, especially the movies.

"If You Want Me, You Get Them"

As noted earlier, Benny Goodman's hiring of pianist Teddy Wilson for his trio in 1935, with the addition of Lionel Hampton on vibes making it a quartet in 1936, broke the color line in popular music. It was particularly noteworthy because Goodman at that time was the hottest thing in show business, not just the music business. Though Goodman hired Wilson and Hampton for musical reasons primarily— in the vernacular of the era, their playing "knocked him out"—the importance of Goodman's decision to do this, a move toward racial desegregation when such moves were extremely rare, cannot be underestimated. Black and white jazz players had played together and recorded together before, to be sure, but playing together in public, regularly, was something else again. "A breakthrough," Wilson called it. "Guys in the music business were telling Benny he'd ruin his career if he hired me," he remembered years later.

The Goodman trio and quartet were a special part of any appearance by the enormously popular Goodman band. Dancers stopped dancing and crowded around the bandstand to hear the Goodman small groups, and the dire consequences predicted by some did not occur. Audiences cheered the trio and quartet.

When a southern hotel owner who had booked the Goodman band discovered Wilson and Hampton would be coming too, he informed Goodman that simply could not be done. Goodman told him: "If you want me, you get them." So they got "them." There were also the traditional problems with restaurants and sleeping accommodations. "South *and* North," said Wilson, adding that Goodman sometimes joined him and Hampton on hotel elevators to avert trouble.

The famous quartet was composed of a Jew whose parents were poverty-stricken immigrants, an ardent Catholic whose mother had hoped he would become a priest (not a drummer of all things), and two quite dissimilar black men: one cool, cultured, and intellectual, the son of Tuskegee College teachers, the other exuberantly down-home despite a big city background, an energetic bundle of smiles and rhythmic stammering grunts when he played, a man who could never be accused of being intellectual. And they played beautifully together, perhaps sending a message that wasn't only musical.

In 1935, Helen Oakley, young jazz writer and later record producer (notably of Ellington small groups), was president of the Chicago Rhythm Club and had much to do with getting Goodman and Wilson to appear together at a jazz concert during Benny's engagement at Chicago's Congress Hotel. This led to Wilson's joining Goodman on a permanent basis. Oakley, who twelve years later married the English jazz critic Stanley Dance, becoming Helen Oakley Dance, may have suggested the major reason why the Goodman trio was created during remarks to Goodman biographer Ross Firestone: "Benny played his best with black musicians like Teddy because most white jazz musicians at that time hadn't caught up yet. In a sense Benny was handicapped playing with his own band, as good as it was, because most of the guys simply weren't on his level. And whenever he worked with black musicians he liked, his own playing became really inspired."

Oakley's point was also eloquently proven later, on the bandstand and in the recording studios, with the 1939–1941 Goodman sextet (actually, seven players including Benny) as the clarinetist played beside Charlie Christian and Cootie Williams, and on such superb recordings as *Gone With What Wind?*, an up-tempo blues, with guest star Count Basie. Similarly, John Hammond contended that Benny was at his incomparable best sharing solos with Lester Young during jam sessions. Goodman, as many one-time Goodman sidemen will be quick to tell you, was never easily impressed, but he was certainly impressed by Lester Young.

Still, in reference to Oakley's comment above, a good many white players did catch up, and it's difficult to imagine Goodman being more inspired than he was when playing, say, with Mel Powell on

Powell's Commodore recording of *The World Is Waiting for the Sunrise,* which identified the clarinetist as "Shoeless John Jackson."

After Wilson and Hampton, Goodman later hired additional black players for his band, as did Charlie Barnet. Cootie Williams joined Goodman in late 1940. Another trumpet player, Peanuts Holland, was with Barnet the following year. Also, in 1941, Roy Eldridge broke up his band, bought out his five-year contract with booker-manager Joe Glaser for one thousand dollars, and joined Gene Krupa. That year, still another star black trumpet player, Hot Lips Page, was featured with the Artie Shaw band. June Richmond sang for a while with Jimmy Dorsey's band before she joined Andy Kirk in 1939. And Billie Holiday was with Shaw in 1938, but she encountered many unpleasant problems that infuriated the singer and Shaw as well. These included being forced to use the freight elevator when the Shaw band was working at the Hotel Lincoln's Blue Room, where she did not sit on the bandstand between songs, as did Shaw's other singer, Helen Forrest. (It was 1943 before a black band, Count Basie's, was hired by the Lincoln.)

The examples of blacks with white bands cited above were exceptions to the rule. Most white band leaders lacked the courage, or something, to hire black players—fearing loss of engagements in top hotels, commercial reprisals of some kind, whatever. Integration in big bands was slow and sparse. No one found it unusual that Woody Herman's "Band That Plays the Blues" had no black players. His later "First Herd," organized in 1945, and "Second Herd," organized in 1947, had a large number of great players but no black players and there was no grumbling about this because it was simply normal practice. When Tommy Dorsey performed and recorded *If the Man in the Moon Were a Coon,* complete with lyrics, during the late 1930s, it inspired few, if any, words of outrage in print. Playing that on the radio now would be unthinkable, and never mind the great saxophone solo by Bud Freeman.

Sometimes Goodman had no black players. Ross Firestone has it right: "Maintaining a racially integrated band was never a cause for Benny as it was for John Hammond, and black musicians came and went like anyone else." Firestone also quotes Mel Powell on this subject: "Benny was one of the very, very few white people I've known who had not a fiber of racism in him. He was absolutely, authentically color-blind, and he thought all the fuss kicked up by the press whenever he hired a black musician was silly. One of the real giveaways to

59

Family Duet—Woody Herman, wife Ingrid, and daughter Charlotte on the December 2, 1946, Down Beat *cover. Like almost every other white band during segregated Swing Era Days, Herman's band had no black players. But Milt Jackson was with Herman by 1949 and blacks were not uncommon in later Herman "Herds." (Reprinted with permission from* Down Beat *magazine.)*

his outlook was that he could be as rude to a black man as to a white man. He did not get patronizing or suddenly gentle. Not at all. And I always found that admirable." A kind of equal opportunity rudeness, you might say.

When the Swing Era was only a memory, I had an interesting chat with John Hammond in 1966 as we listened to a Goodman sextet at New York's Rainbow Grill, located on the sixty-forth floor of

Rockefeller Center, as is the more famous Rainbow Room. This was a lively Goodman group, thanks in large measure to trumpet player Doc Cheatham, who was lead trumpet player in Cab Calloway's band when I was a kid, and the expert pianist Hank Jones. I said to John: "This is a nice little integrated band Benny has here. I notice that the drummer [Morey Feld] is white." Hammond thought this remark was hilarious, laughing while saying, "I've got to tell Benny what you said because he probably hadn't even noticed that!"

In his delightful autobiography *Those Swinging Years,* Charlie Barnet said that even before Goodman hired Wilson, "Benny Carter would sometimes sit in with our trumpet section. The lighting [in that club] was such that nobody could tell who was sitting there."

Barnet also hired the beautiful Lena Horne to sing with his band in 1940. He worried about taking her south but discovered in Knoxville that they "chose to think she was an Indian. I guess they thought nobody would be rash enough to bring a black girl along with a white band."

Sounding like Goodman, Barnet also said: "I never made a point of hiring black musicians to change the social order. I hired them because of how well they played, not with the idea of starting a racial revolution." Barnet went on to have as many as five black musicians in his band at one time, including Oscar Pettiford (born on an Indian reservation in Oklahoma), Trummy Young, and Dick Vance. Two truly great trumpet players, Charlie Shavers and Clark Terry, later worked for Barnet.

When Barnet was billed as "The White Ellington," a misnomer, I discovered just how much his music appealed to those who were not white when I gave up trying to see his band at the Howard Theater in Washington one weekday afternoon after high school. I had seen this Barnet band shortly before—at Atlantic City's Steel Pier ballroom, where the sheer volume of Cliff Leeman's cymbal-crashing took my breath away—and the lines to see Barnet, on T Street in front of the Howard, were much too long. This amazed me because I had never stood in line to get into the Howard to see greater bands than Barnet had, including those of Ellington, Basie, and Lunceford. Barnet's band was the only white one, in my memory, to play the Howard before I entered the Army in February 1943. It came as no surprise to discover, in Barnet's autobiography, that he not only led the first white band to play the Apollo in Harlem (at Benny Carter's suggestion) but that he broke the house record there. "This success brought in other black theaters," Barnet recalled, "which became a private gold mine for me," and one of those theaters was the Howard.

During the Swing Era, blacks and whites swung together in small groups on Fifty-second Street and elsewhere. Trumpet player Red Allen's career encompassed much jazz history, from his father's brass band in New Orleans to Fate Marable and the Mississippi riverboats, then on to King Oliver, Fletcher Henderson, and the Mills Blue Rhythm Band ("take your trumpet from your side, and *Ride, Red, Ride* ... goodness gracious, you thrill me bodacious, so ride, ride, ride, Red, ride!"). For younger readers who may wonder, the word "ride" was a popular term for soloing, improvising, swinging, which Allen did with gusto. And making still more jazz history, in 1936 it was the presence of Red Allen that made a Joe Marsala group at the Hickory House the first regular "mixed" band on Fifty-second Street.

Black faces were, however, rare in white big bands. Willie Smith, one of the great alto saxophone players, a standout with Jimmie Lunceford for more than ten years, was with the white bands of Charlie Spivak in 1941, and after time in the Navy, Harry James in 1944. But Smith looked more white than black, could have "passed" if he had so desired, and this may have been one reason he was hired by Spivak and James.

Jimmy Dorsey was quick to praise his friend Goodman for hiring black musicians. (When neither had a band, they were roommates and the first of the two to answer the phone got the recording date or gig for a clarinetist or alto saxophone player.) But Dorsey said he could not hire black players as Goodman did and succeed financially, which may or may not have been true. The idea was that Goodman, "The King of Swing," was so popular he could do whatever he wanted, Dorsey and others could not. Unlike his trombonist brother Tommy, noted for a gorgeous tone, temper tantrums, and running a taut ship, Jimmy was enormously well liked by his sidemen, and considered to be one of the kindest, fairest leaders in the business. Perhaps he simply liked his band the way it was and did not want the hassles a mixed band would bring, who knows?

It is pointless and almost impossible to rehash or explain with any degree of certainty all the slippery slopes of racial thinking then. It is similarly a major mistake to view such Swing Era situations from a perspective dated decades after the Supreme Court's 1954 decision on *Brown v. Board of Education,* correcting the Court's 1896 "separate but equal" ruling, and the civil rights movement that followed.

What is sometimes called "presentism" in academic circles, meaning the application of contemporary standards to the past, and described by historian Douglas L. Wilson as an "inability to make appropriate allowances for prevailing historical conditions," is always dangerous. The fact is that segregation was everywhere during the Swing Era. And even if jazz band integration could and should have been wider, jazz music during the Swing Era did much to break down color lines, to clear the way for desegregation. Jazz music certainly did much more than any other musical or dramatic area of show business, high-brow or lowbrow, including the stage, the movies, symphony orchestras, radio studios, opera, or burlesque.

There is reason for this: most white jazz musicians have always felt differently than many other white people about race, simply because it is tough, if not impossible, to idolize someone like Louis Armstrong and be prejudiced against him at the same time. Bud Freeman spoke for many young white Chicago kids discovering the joys of jazz during the 1920s when he said his musical education came from South Side clubs where he heard Bessie Smith, Jimmie Noone, Earl Hines, and other great players. He also recalled that "blacks treated me beautifully."

How Freeman, Jimmy McPartland, Muggsy Spanier, Dave Tough, Benny Goodman, Gene Krupa, and other teenaged white jazz-happy Chicago kids were treated in black clubs during the 1920s reminds me of how I was treated in Washington's black clubs during the Swing Era. I was obviously an "ofay," pig Latin for "foe" and common lingo for white guy then, but I never felt like a foe nor was I treated like one during all my countless hours listening to jazz in black clubs and ballrooms in Washington when it was a segregated city. How segregated was the nation's capital then? About the only white restaurant in Washington that would serve blacks was the one in Union Station. White high school sports teams did not play even practice games against black high school teams.

I was always among a small minority of whites in black clubs and ballrooms. There were, for example, fewer than a half-dozen whites present when I discovered the glories of the marvelous Jimmie Lunceford reed section in a ballroom beneath the Lincoln Theater on U Street before World War II. This was the same ballroom where Rex Stewart first heard live jazz in 1921.

At the Howard, Washington's Apollo, there was always a smattering of whites admiring the swing bands and top dancers, including

63

*Distinctively Different—The Jimmie Lunceford Orchestra, as shown here
playing in a Detroit club in 1940, was one of the best and most easily
identified of all big bands. Players shown, from left to right, are trumpeters
Paul Webster, Snooky Young, and Ted Buckner, tenor saxophonist Joe Thomas,
and leader Lunceford. (Copyright Frank Driggs Collection.)*

the kid with the Will Mastin Trio, Sammy Davis Jr. And I remember seeing a high school student like me, Don Lamond, studiously
watching how Jo Jones did it when the Basie band was in town.
Don became one of Woody Herman's finest drummers in 1945,
and drummer-critic Goodman considered him to be one of the
best ever.

In later years, after the war, at small places such as the Club Bengasi,
where few whites were to be found and where the bandstand didn't
even face most of the customers, I was a regular patron, continuously
learning more about jazz, including not to come to the Bengasi on
an opening night by Lester Young. I did that once and was told sorry,
Lester had been "hung up" by an afternoon jam session in Baltimore.

All this was decades before violent crime was an everyday occur-
rence in Washington, before the major invasion of heroin, the later

cheaper crack cocaine, and robbery and murder, sometimes random, by young addicts and dope peddlers in some areas of our nation's capital city.

Another Form of Prejudice

During the Swing Era, segregation, in countless ways that were sometimes legal, sometimes illegal but habitual, made certain that racial prejudice overwhelmed other prejudices, including but not limited to anti-Semitism. But unofficial segregation and prejudice within black communities, based on skin color and so-called social class, also existed. The inhuman outrage of slavery was long gone, but whites unquestionably had infinitely more advantages and opportunities to succeed than blacks had, whatever their shade. Still, many lighter-skinned blacks had advantages and opportunities that many darker-skinned blacks did not.

Unlike light-tan Cotton Club chorus lines, black jazz bands were not involved with skin color favoritism. Players were hired and judged by the content of their musicianship, not by the color of their skin. There was black, brown, and beige in Ellington's band, and a valve trombonist, Juan Tizol, born in Puerto Rico, looked lighter than beige. The same was true of other "colored" or "Negro" bands, as they were then described. "Afro-American" was the name of a newspaper, and calling anyone an African American would have been met with a response of shock and anger. Nor was "black" used then as it is now. As Cab Calloway said: "Our people were colored or Negro, never black. To call me black was a triple insult … . I've always accepted the fact that I'm Negro … . Even black people have given me a hard way to go sometimes. They've called me a dirty yeller and poor white. That went on for years in the thirties and forties. Some people were bothered because they thought I was Cuban or Puerto Rican. It's a horrible thing when people want to classify you or resort to name calling."

In jazz, there have been color lines of different shades dating back to New Orleans before World War I. In early jazz days, Creoles who were descended from Spanish and French ancestry and who took pride in reading music often looked down on darker American Negro players such as clarinetist Johnny Dodds who did not read music. And during the 1920s, up north in Chicago, a city that had scarred itself with a horrible race riot in 1919, there was a so-called boundary line that Negro musicians could not cross to find employment. According to clarinetist Barney Bigard, "if we tried to take a job in a white place then, Petrillo would send the goons in," sometimes with bombs. Bigard was referring to the late 1920s when he was with King Oliver's band and when James C. Petrillo, later national kingpin of the American Federation of Musicians, headed Chicago's white musicians' local. And during the Swing Era, there were separate black and white musicians' unions in most cities, including Washington and Los Angeles, and this alone served to keep integration in jazz bands down simply because a bandleader would hire musicians from his own local.

Although some view racial prejudice as an either-or, white versus black problem with no gray (or brown) areas, racial prejudice has always been more complicated than that. The problem has involved white, and—to borrow a 1944 Ellington suite title—black, brown, and beige.

Though not a happening to be confused with The Golden Rule or The Way Things Ought to Be, it is understandable how a nation composed of people with ancestors of different colors, religions, and nationalities, who then mixed in our melting pot in many different ways, could create an assortment of bedeviling color and class problems along the way. Even today, despite all the jargon about the joys of diversity and multiethnicity, many people insist upon viewing U.S. citizens not as individual Americans but as members of some kind of hyphenated subgroup.

It may be of more than passing interest to note that Andy Razaf's compelling lyrics in ("What did I do to be so") *Black and Blue*, involved racial prejudice within what was then called the Negro race. Introduced by singer Edith Wilson on Broadway in the 1929 show *Hot Chocolates,* the verse reads, in part:

> *Black, and 'cause I'm black I'm blue.*
> *Browns and yellers all have fellers,*
> *Gentlemen prefer them light,*
> *Wish I could fade, can't make the grade.*

And the first chorus begins, "Cold empty bed, springs hard as lead ... . No joys for me, no company ... ."

Barry Singer, in his excellent 1992 biography of Razaf, stresses "the power those lyrics gained from Leonard Harper's strikingly theatrical staging of the song ... the jet black Edith Wilson was revealed to the audience on an all-white set in a white satin gown, lying amid white satin bedclothes on an enormous white bed."

As usually presented and understood today and for many years, *Black and Blue* is only about white prejudice against blacks. But Singer wisely suggests "the difficulties for women of a truly black pigment to attract a good black man" was "an initial deceptive thrust ... of a song whose lyric chorus quickly revealed itself to be far more pointed toward the universal plight of the black race within white society."

Skin color prejudices once found in black communities are well presented in two of the best autobiographies by jazz musicians, *Boy Meets Horn* by cornetist Rex Stewart, with Ellington for ten years, and *Bass Line* by bass player Milt Hinton, with Calloway for fifteen years. (Hinton's book also has many excellent photos by the author, including one of Calloway band members in front of the "colored entrance" to the Atlanta railroad station circa 1940). Both men describe this other kind of prejudice, as it hit them as teenagers in the 1920s, when Stewart was growing up in Washington, and Hinton in Chicago.

Hinton remembered that "light-complected people seemed to feel that they were better or higher class than other blacks," light-skinned models were always used in advertisements, "and even though nobody ever said it out loud, the message given out to blacks was pretty clear—you'll get ahead in the world if you look as white as you can."

Stewart remembered that Washington "had clear distinctions between colored versus white people, and, more important to me, the indisputable differentiation between Negro people of various hues. There was little mixing in the homes, in the churches or in the dance halls."

The cornetist grew up in the oldest part of Washington, Georgetown, long before it was called "fashionable Georgetown," and his skin was not light. He did not go to what was then black Washington's elite, selective Dunbar High School where it was easier for those with lighter skin and a comfortable economic situation to be admitted, and where graduates usually went on to college and sometimes to national political, academic, or scientific prominence.

What Stewart discovered in the 1920s remained the same, more or less, during the 1930s and throughout the Swing Era. It was all part of the skin color approach to humanity. And even long after the Swing Era, in 1957, some of us wondered this: Would enormously popular singer-pianist Nat Cole have been able to find a national sponsor for his excellent TV program if his shade had been as light as, say, that of Senator Edward Brooke, one of Dunbar High School's famous graduates? So, some will insist it is different now.

To understand this aspect of the Swing Era, one should remember the gangster-run Cotton Club in Harlem was where the Ellington and Calloway bands held sway before the Swing Era arrived. The Cotton Club was for white patrons. Bouncers at the door permitted only a tiny handful of black celebrities to enter. Calloway, whose band followed Ellington's at the Cotton Club in 1930, remembers that "the whole set was like the sleepy-time-down South during slavery ... the idea was to make whites who came feel like they were being catered to and entertained by black slaves."

Until 1936, the Cotton Club was located at 142nd Street and Lenox Avenue. When a large housing development in that block began, the club moved from uptown to downtown at Forty-eighth and Broadway. And the Cotton Club was known for more than music. It proudly advertised its "copper colored gals" and its musical shows had such titles as *Brown Sugar—Sweet but Unrefined* (music by Harold Arlen). Lena Horne, a light-skinned, teenaged beauty—in the slang of the time, "a beginner brown"—fit right in as one of the club's copper-colored chorines, working three shows a night, seven nights a week for twenty-five dollars. Even if it is believed that the chorus was "copper colored" because of its white patrons, lighter skin was preferred by many Negro audiences, too. And those described by such strange terms as mulatto, quadroon, or octoroon did have certain advantages, even though this was when, it must be remembered, many otherwise sane people actually believed that "one drop of blood" by an ancestor could make one legally Negro and therefore legally disadvantaged.

The craziness of all this racial categorizing is stressed in Lena Horne's excellent 1965 autobiography *Lena*. She recalled a dinner date she had with singer Billy Daniels, a popular singer in Fifty-second Street clubs long before he became a supper club and Ed Sullivan TV program favorite: "Billy Daniels is a very fair-skinned man and when we went to a restaurant once we were asked to leave because I was too dark. They thought Billy was a white man taking a Negro woman into a place where they were not allowed."

And John Hammond in his autobiography remembered an interesting event in the life of Earle Warren, lead alto saxophone player in Basie's greatest band: "When the [Basie] band arrived in either

Hopkinsville or Owensboro, Kentucky—can't remember which—members of the band noticed that Earle Warren, the handsome new lead alto, was jittery. The reason soon became clear when a deputy sheriff arrived at the dance hall to order him out of town for sitting in with a 'nigger band.' It seems that light-skinned Earle had led an all-white group there four months earlier and was assumed to be white himself."

As for the other way around, a white passing in a black band, there were no doubt others, but the only musician I ever knew who did it was Washington trumpet player Kenny Fulcher. At age nineteen, while he had his own college band during the 1940s in his hometown of Roanoke, Virginia, he also played in an otherwise all-Negro swing band led by Gene Jones, a drummer like his brother Slick Jones, who played for Fats Waller. Fulcher was lead trumpet, also took the jazz solos, and as the only white member of this band there were problems. After his presence inspired a few fights in the audience, he took his mother's advice: "She told me to put some sun tan powder on and let my hair grow. I did, and I passed pretty well."

During the 1950s and early 1960s, while holding down a government job, Fulcher worked three nights a week in pianist Booker Coleman's "mixed" band (Kenny was often the only one mixing it) at Washington's Charles Hotel Lounge, a basement club in a small black hotel. Kenny was a commanding player who excelled in the upper register, able to hit an F or G above high C and stay there, "warming up those notes a bit," as did Bunny Berigan. And he used a legitimate mouthpiece, not a pea-shooter, unlike some much more famous players known for high-register skill. Perhaps the fact that he needed crutches to get around gave him his barrel chest and great lung strength. Kenny and his wife were later killed in a horrible automobile crash. Like so many other talented musicians who remained in cities other than New York, Chicago, or Los Angeles, only a tiny handful of the thousands who might have enjoyed his playing ever heard him play.

It is easy to understand why some black jazz players resented the fame and financial success of some Swing Era bandleaders and sidemen. "They make more money than I do although I play better"—that was the idea. Another common complaint: "They can get jobs that I can't get, in radio studios and elsewhere." A banner headline-in-red-ink story on the May 1, 1943, front page of *Down Beat* reported: "The first Negro musician ever engaged to play with a white orchestra on a network [radio] program originating in Hollywood played one show and was dropped without notice due to a 'request' issued from some undisclosed source." The musician was drummer Lee Young, Lester Young's younger brother. The conductor who hired him told Lee he had done a fine job and that he was engaged regularly for the show, which was to run for thirteen weeks. But when he appeared the next week, the contractor told him he had been "requested" to get somebody else, and a white drummer was already on hand to work the show. Just what happened remained mysterious, as often happened in such situations then.

Meanwhile, in New York the year before, pianist Raymond Scott had led the first "mixed" radio studio orchestra specializing in jazz on CBS, a band that included Charlie Shavers and Ben Webster. And the year before that, in 1941, that marvelous piano player on the popular CBS show *Casey, Crime Photographer* was Herman Chittison. Of course this was radio, not television, and Chittison was heard, not seen.

After World War II, Pearl Bailey and Billie Holiday numbered among the major crowd pleasers at the 2011 Club in the basement of Washington's biggest black hotel, the Hotel Dunbar, a hotel much needed then when segregation meant whites-only in fancier downtown hotels. It was at the 2011 where Nat Cole, a gentleman whose musicianship, like himself, epitomized good taste and true class, introduced me to his new young bride, Maria. Forty-plus years later, I read this quote by their daughter, singer Natalie Cole: "For a dark-skinned man like my father to acquire a light-skinned woman such as my mother was a real important prize. Your status moved up. That doesn't mean that her family was all that happy about her marrying my father. He was too black for them."

So there it was again, a reminder of that other kind of racial prejudice, not white-black but something in-between, which I knew about but which had certainly not crossed my mind when I chatted with just-married Mr. and Mrs. Cole at the 2011 Club. And it came from Natalie Cole, someone who did not exist then.

After the Swing Era was over, Tommy Dorsey, Woody Herman, and a few others who had led all-white bands during the Swing Era, did have a few black players from time to time. But this was long after the fight had more or less been won, with the color line blurred. And Count Basie's post–Swing Era band, his crack "arrangers band" (the one-more-time *April in Paris* band) eventually had a few white players.

One was trumpet player Paul Cohen, who sometimes played lead trumpet, and this was understandable because it wasn't easy finding any player of any shade who could cut the tough Basie charts as Paul Cohen could. By this time, the late 1950s, bandstand racial restrictions, real or only perceived to be real, were winding down. Soon no one found it odd when white whiz-bang drummer Butch Miles added flashy rhythmic wallop to the Basie jazz machine.

It's About Artistry, Not Race

In recent years, jazz has often been presented as a black art, or African-American art. There are those, including some who receive considerable attention in the press, who seem to be saying that white men not only can't jump but can't really play jazz, can't truly swing, because they do not have the required soul or something. It has also been suggested that contributions to jazz by white players have been meager. But such suggestions are absurd, clearly based on some sort of racial militancy unrelated to music, as accomplished black and white jazz musicians well know or surely should know.

Some younger musicians today may have been taught jazz history differently, thus all the Crow Jim (opposite of Jim Crow) posturing, but who can imagine Louis Armstrong putting down Bunny Berigan or Jack Teagarden? Or Oscar Peterson putting down his guitarists Barney Kessel, Herb Ellis, or Joe Pass? Don't tell Peterson that any of those three could not play jazz music extremely well. Can anyone imagine Duke Ellington suggesting that Louis Bellson, whose drumming did so much to enliven the Ellington band when it most needed enlivening, ain't got that swing? Could anyone who knows anything about jazz seriously suggest that the ghost of Count Basie might say that Zoot Sims lacked sufficient "soul" to swing? How do those who insist that jazz is only a black art explain away the obvious jazz artistry of Urbie Green, Dave McKenna, and Jimmie Rowles? Don't tell Lionel Hampton, swinger extraordinaire, that Benny Goodman didn't swing, and Vic Dickenson would have been shocked if anyone questioned Bobby Hackett's jazz spirit. But there is no need to list even a tiny handful of the many standout white jazz players who most certainly did and do swing.

Jazz is not defined by race but by artistry. Dave Tough could not have been a greater drummer had he been black, brown, beige, or octoroon. Would Willie Smith have swung more if he had been darker?

Swing Vibes Champion—Lionel Hampton graces the cover of the September 1, 1943, issue of Down Beat. *(Reprinted with permission from* Down Beat *magazine.)*

Without the American Negro there would have been no jazz as we know it, that's certain, and most of the great jazz innovators have been black. But jazz artistry is not determined by how innovative a musician may be. Originality is not the only thing that counts, although jazz critics, especially, have tended to overemphasize innovation, as if what's new and different is of primary and overwhelming importance. Like any other artistic activity, the truth is that performance is more important than innovation. Were Rembrandt, Degas, and Daumier major innovators? Maybe not, but they were surely major artists.

A few salient facts: some great jazz players have been white, white players have inspired black players as well as the more common other way around, jazz harmonies did not come from Africa, and the jazz beat is quite different from the drum beats in Africa. Also, jazz did not exist in Africa. Jazz was born and bred in America.

It may be understandable why some black activists insist that white men stole their music and only black people have what it takes to play real jazz, but it simply isn't true, as thousands of recordings made before, during, and after the Swing Era prove. Crow Jim is as wrong as Jim Crow. However it began, jazz is American music, not African-American music.

Bud Freeman had it right: "You don't have to be white to be corny."

Benny Carter also had it right: "You don't have to be black to play jazz. And, if you are black, it doesn't mean you can swing."

Swinging on Fifty-second Street—Part of the marvelous Count Basie Band in action at the Famous Door on New York's Fifty-second Street ("Swing Alley") in July 1938. Guitarist is Freddie Green. Trumpet players, from left, are Buck Clayton, Ed Lewis, and Harry "Sweets" Edison. (Copyright Frank Driggs Collection.)

3
Dozens of
Great Players

"You'd be surprised how many people I run into who've never heard of Art Tatum or Teddy Wilson."

—Pianist Ray Bryant, 1978

MORE THAN FIFTY YEARS after guitarist Steve Jordan at age twenty went on the road with the Will Bradley-Ray McKinley orchestra, the first of nine "name bands" he played in, he said this: "The real golden age of jazz, when there were many great players and all able to get work, too, was the Swing Era … . Perhaps I feel this way because I am of that generation. But to my mind, when the big bands were cooking, when Fifty-second Street meant music, was when it was really happening. There were dozens, maybe hundreds, of exciting young players then. Don't tell me that's true today."

Dozens of exciting young players. Without question. For example, the man who revolutionized bass playing and made it a fascinating solo instrument, Jimmy Blanton, was only eighteen when he joined Ellington. Pianist Mel Powell was playing with Bobby Hackett at age sixteen and two years later was celebrating the ways of Teddy Wilson and Earl Hines, as well as the original ways of Mel Powell, with

Goodman. Tenor saxophonist Georgie Auld, in his teens while with the bands of Bunny Berigan and Artie Shaw, had improved markedly by age twenty-one, having learned his Hawkins lessons well, and was holding his own in Goodman's finest sextet. Illinois Jacquet was nineteen when he began to drive crowds into gleeful frenzy with sensational and some said "erotic" solos for Lionel Hampton's band in 1941.

Trombonist Urbie Green was on the road with big bands at age sixteen, which was the age of Israel Crosby when this exceptional bass player recorded *Blues of Israel*. Billy Butterfield was only twenty when he joined Bob Crosby's band, and fleet-fingered pianist Joey Bushkin was working on Fifty-second Street and in big bands while still in his teens. (Aside: Has anyone, anywhere, at any time, ever played *California, Here I Come* more swingingly than Bushkin did?) Louis Bellson was Goodman's drummer at age nineteen.

Art Pepper was seventeen when he was with a Benny Carter band in Los Angeles, and eighteen when he joined Stan Kenton in 1943. Pepper became one of the most exciting of all alto saxophone players in the post–Swing Era despite a serious heroin addiction and much jail time (Pepper described himself frankly as "a dope fiend" in his searing autobiography *Straight Life*). And his best playing, whether influenced by the innovations of Charlie Parker or not, always contained the emotional and lyrical spirit of the pre-bop Swing Era. Indeed, his *Straight Life* up-tempo piece, as anyone familiar with songs favored by Swing Era players immediately recognizes, is based on the chord progression of *After You've Gone*. Had Pepper been born later, with no Swing Era roots, he no doubt would not have played the way he did.

There were dozens of exciting older players cooking during the Swing Era, too. A history of jazz that excluded musicians active during the Swing Era would be impossible, or simply a meaningless book. A ton of great players were active then, many more great ones than ever before. Or since. Let's recall only several dozen of these, with emphasis on major players, beginning with Louis Armstrong.

Beauty, Truth, Armstrong

Who can say how many kids discovered jazz because of Louis Armstrong? Thousands? Millions? The number is beyond estimation. "Beauty is truth," wrote John Keats, and for me an unforgettable

78

The Major Jazz Hero—Great trumpet player Louis Armstrong, who inspired and influenced most of the prominent Swing Era jazz musicians, seems to be making quite a fashion statement as he poses in London in 1933, shortly before the start of the Swing Era. (Copyright Frank Driggs Collection.)

discovery of truth came the first time I heard the sound of Armstrong's trumpet (on a 1932 Victor recording of *That's My Home,* using a nonelectric, windup phonograph). I played his solo, which moved breathtakingly into the upper register, over and over again. Such an experience involving beauty, truth, and Louis Armstrong was not uncommon. He turned many into jazz enthusiasts. As Charlie Barnet's autobiography reported: "I still think the first night I heard him was the most exciting thing that ever happened to me musically." Barnet's view was typical of many who became prominent jazz players during the Swing Era.

During the 1920s, Louis Armstrong was *the* jazz musician's jazz musician. In a way, all jazz players play Louis. More than anyone else, he altered jazz from an ensemble-band music to a soloist's art as well. Despite all the acclaim properly given to Ellington and other jazz orchestrators and composers, jazz has always been primarily a player's art, and Louis Armstrong was unquestionably one of its greatest players. During the Swing Era, he was still playing extremely well but was often found fronting a big band of mediocre musicians or recording with non-peers.

Many have attempted to explain the greatness of Armstrong. Teddy Wilson, who played in an Armstrong band before joining Goodman (Teddy found it amazing how Louis "could play so well with such a bad band behind him"), may have explained Armstrong's greatness as well as anyone. Asked by this writer during an interview for *Down Beat* in 1958 to sum up his feelings about Armstrong, Wilson said:

I think Louis is the greatest jazz musician that's ever been. He had a combination of all the factors that make a good musician. He had balance ... this most of all. Tone. Harmonic sense. Excitement. Technical skill. Originality. Every musician, no matter how good, usually has something out of balance, be it tone, too much imitativeness, or whatever. But in Armstrong everything was in balance. He had no weak point. Of course, I am speaking in terms of the general idiom of his day. I don't think there has been a musician since Armstrong who has had all the factors in balance, all the factors equally developed. Such a balance was the essential thing about Beethoven, I think, and Armstrong, like Beethoven, had this high development of balance. Lyricism. Delicacy. Emotional outburst. Rhythm. Complete mastery of his horn.

Armstrong was also the greatest of all jazz singers, and his appeal was not limited to musicians and jazz music fans. His love of entertaining people, and great ability to do so, could be understood by any garden variety of square. Once a poor boy who sang on the streets of New Orleans for pennies before learning cornet in the city's Waifs Home, Armstrong brought great artistry and joy to the world. Dizzy Gillespie said it well a year before Armstrong's death in 1971. During a Newport Jazz Festival program on Armstrong, Dizzy said: "Louis Armstrong's station in the history of jazz is unimpeachable. If it hadn't been for him, there wouldn't be none of us. I thank Mr. Louis Armstrong for my livelihood."

Armstrong was a major jazz figure before, during, and after the Swing Era. And he influenced, directly or indirectly, every jazz trumpet player of the Swing Era.

Despite Armstrong's mighty presence, Roy Eldridge and Bunny Berigan were probably *the* trumpet players of the Swing Era.

They called Roy Eldridge "Little Jazz." The nickname was appropriate because he was small in stature and he was jazz as much as any man ever was. Eldridge was influenced by Armstrong, and Dizzy Gillespie was influenced by Eldridge, jazz authorities keep saying. And it's true, in a way, but is essentially misleading when it leaves the impression that Eldridge was only some kind of "link," as one jazz critic strangely said, between Louis and Dizzy. The truth is that Eldridge was much too great a player, with too much individuality, to be downgraded into any kind of "link" between any other famous players.

Eldridge was Eldridge and no one played like Eldridge but Eldridge. Excitement was his game and he was all over his horn, excelling in all registers. His driving improvisations majored in snap, crackle, and pop. Eldridge did not doodle around on the trumpet. He played with strength and conviction, thriving on musical challenges. His enthusiasm for music, not the music business, was constant. He was the catalyst, the spark, and the star of a thousand jam sessions. He told me he liked hear a note on the trumpet crack like a whip, and few could whip-crack notes the way Roy could. He had no trouble moving from a raucous, dirty-sounding lower register to a shiny, sparkling-clean upper register.

The musical daredeviltry of Eldridge—his reach sometimes exceeded his grasp—is remembered, too. In a 1994 newspaper column, writer Nat Hentoff recalled how jazz promoter and record producer Norman

Granz answered an *Izveystia* reporter in Russia when he was asked which musician most typifies jazz: "Without hesitating, he named the trumpet player Roy Eldridge. 'He's a musician for whom it's far more important to dare, to try to achieve a particular peak—even if he falls on his ass in the attempt—than it is to play safe. That's what jazz is all about.' "

Like Eldridge, Bunny Berigan mastered all registers, and dug deeper into the lower register, habitually, than other players did. In the upper register, he remained lyrical, not showboatingly sensational. He had a big, powerful tone throughout his horn. His solos could be breathtaking and his original melodic ideas—his famous solo on Tommy Dorsey's *Marie* is a good example—seemed boundless.

Cootie Williams was another important Swing Era trumpet star, with Ellington throughout the 1930s and with the Goodman band and Benny's finest sextet for a year, 1940–1941, before leading his own band. Widely known for his "growl" plunger work, as on *Concerto for Cootie* and other Ellington pieces, Cootie was an exceptional all-around player, able to bring Armstrong to mind on open horn. Goodman once said Williams was the best trumpet player he ever had, and he certainly had some fine ones, including Berigan.

Charlie Shavers could do it all. Inspired by Armstrong as were many others, he developed a distinctive style and was easy to identify on a record, whether using a mute or playing open horn. Shavers had amazing technical skill, a fine tone, great range, classic precision. He could roar and he could whisper. Also an arranger, he created the sound of the John Kirby combo, and *Undecided* was his most widely known composition.

Bobby Hackett, who idolized Armstrong but was often compared to cornetist Bix Beiderbecke because of Bobby's lyrical approach and absolutely lovely cornet tone, was another remarkable player. A guitarist before he took up cornet, he later switched to English cornet, which he told me "looks more like a trumpet, so they call me a trumpet player." Harmonic knowledge was always apparent in his playing and no doubt his guitar background helped him here because to play decent straight rhythm guitar you must necessarily know chord changes and harmonic ins and outs. Hackett worked with Eddie Condon groups and had a reputation of being a Dixielander at one time, but his always melodic playing was never easily categorized. On ballads he was almost beyond compare. Some of Hackett's solos were like a warm and gentle kiss that lingers in the mind, and heart.

Count Basie's first and greatest band (*One O'clock Jump, Swingin' the Blues, Every Tub, Doggin' Around,* et al.) included two superb trumpet players, Buck Clayton and Harry "Sweets" Edison. Clayton was always a joy to hear. Known for his cup mute work as well as his crisp, no-nonsense open horn, Buck was also an able arranger. Edison brought great humor to his rhythmically driving solos and certainly had his own way of phrasing. He often repeated a phrase several times with a slightly different accent and volume each time, bringing smiles to all who were hip. Like Clayton, Edison made joyously crystal clear his compulsion to swing. Lester Young, who gave Billie Holiday her "Lady Day" title, reportedly is the one who named him "Sweets."

Cornetist Rex Stewart, one of the stars of the Ellington band, was known for his half-valve tricks involving not-quite-notes on *Boy Meets Horn,* and was a thoughtful, versatile player. His small group recordings with other Ellington players have withstood the test of time and will withstand other tests any jazz historian of the future may dream up. Stewart was also a delightful and articulate gentleman to talk to, as his fine essays on jazz suggest.

Ray Nance, who replaced Cootie Williams in the Ellington band in 1940 *(When Cootie Left the Duke)* had a fat tone and could he swing! Played violin, sang, and danced, too. There are many fine Nance solos on Ellington recordings, one of the best known on the original 1941 version of Billy Strayhorn's *Take the 'A' Train,* the subway train that goes to Harlem.

Muggsy Spanier, still another who idolized Armstrong as a young man, was a big favorite with those who preferred what was called traditional jazz. With his forceful use of the plunger mute, the word "driving" was customarily used to describe a Spanier solo. His sixteen "Ragtime Band" small group recordings on Bluebird in 1939 were cherished by many, and understandably so.

Max Kaminsky, Yank Lawson, Jimmy McPartland, and Wild Bill Davison were among the best of other white trumpet players usually associated with traditional or "Dixieland" groups during the Swing Era. Kaminsky and Lawson also played in prominent big bands. Davison's cornet, as Dan Morgenstern wrote, could be lyrical or raunchy, and he could "push any band, no matter how sluggish, into some semblance of drive." When Wild Bill came from Milwaukee to New York in 1941, Eddie Condon surely viewed him as one of the greatest joys discovered since a way was found to distill a fermented mash of grain into booze.

Harry James was probably the most widely known of all Swing Era trumpet players. From 1936–1938, he was the most featured soloist in the Goodman band aside from Goodman, and he picked up many more fans after organizing his own band in 1939. James had bewildering technical skill and could swing, too, but became immensely popular for vibrato-laced, almost cloyingly sweet ballad work. This brought home the bacon for Harry but the way he played *You Made Me Love You* didn't cut it with jazz purists. Nor did Harry's more sensational display of skill on *Flight of the Bumblebee*. Overrated by some, perhaps, and underrated by others, James was no mere "circus" player although his tone did seem a bit razzy when compared to some other notable Swing Era players. Still, many superior musicians held him in extremely high regard. Perhaps his jazz playing, like the jazz playing of many, was a matter of taste.

Another trumpet player from the first Goodman band, Atlantic City's Ziggy Elman (aka Harry Finkelman) received considerable attention. A Yiddish *fralich* bit that began his *And the Angels Sing* solo helped to make him famous with Goodman, and he was featured even more during his half-dozen years with Tommy Dorsey. Ziggy's brash, rip-roaring solos were crowd-pleasers, and extrovert Ziggy was a frequent jazz poll winner.

One the great trumpet players of the Swing Era, in big and small bands, was Billy Butterfield. He had a full, clear ringing tone and as much power as anyone after Berigan reached the Pearly Gates. "Butterball," as his colleagues called this short, chubby man, was obviously inspired by Armstrong, but unlike many others who were, his rich tone was not diminished in any way when he tooled into the upper register that Louis once almost totally owned.

Some lead trumpet players, such as Harry James, were also solo stars, but lead trumpet players who did not solo much did not get the attention "hot chair" players did. These lead players were immensely important to swing bands, however, and were often more highly paid than the better-known soloists. Among the best lead trumpeters: Doc Cheatham (with Calloway and more briefly with Wilson and Carter), Snookie Young (Lunceford, Basie, Hampton, Carter), and Jimmy Maxwell (Goodman).

"Big Tea," Musician's Musician

The jazz trombone may have started as a kind of rhythm instrument in New Orleans and elsewhere, but by the late 1920s—thanks to such players as Miff Mole, Jimmy Harrison (dead by age thirty in 1931), and Jack Teagarden—the trombone had become a major melodic jazz instrument. By the Swing Era, it was one of the most compelling jazz horns, and Teagarden was its most admired master.

Teagarden was a musician's musician with an ability to play chorus after chorus at any tempo with unflagging invention. Having Teagarden on a record date or at a jam session was considered a special event by the other musicians involved. Yes, I, too, have heard those maddening words "you should have been here last night, Big Tea sat in!"

Better known to the general public than some other jazz giants, partly because of his years with Paul Whiteman, Teagarden was enormously popular with jazz musicians of all schools. And he inspired no jealousy, as did some other famous players. The most famous trombone player in the nation, Tommy Dorsey, was always quick to disparage his own jazz playing when it was compared, by the unaware, to the playing of Teagarden.

The "bone" is not an easy instrument to play well, demanding an embouchure (how lips and tongue are used on a mouthpiece) of strength and flexibility plus skilled control of its seven slide positions, but Teagarden made playing the trombone seem natural and simple. He brought relaxation, ease, and virility to jazz trombone. The big Texan, who looked part Indian but said he was not, also did what few white men have been able to do well: sing the blues with conviction, with heart.

Teagarden signed a five-year contract with Whiteman in 1933, and this kept him from considering a chair in Goodman's first band as Benny had hoped and delayed organization of his own band until the Swing Era was well along. His big band had only moderate success.

Among other exciting Swing Era trombonists: Dicky Wells with Basie, Vic Dickenson with Basie later, Trummy Young with Lunceford, and Lawrence Brown with Ellington were all exceptional and quite different. The improvisations of Wells and Young were enlivened by humor, sometimes broad, sometimes sly. Brown was a smooth, classy, impeccable performer who batted in the same major league as Tommy Dorsey and Jack Jenney when it came to ballad time. Benny Morton also cannot be forgotten. He was one of the best all-around big band (Henderson, Redman, Basie, and Carter) and small band (even Condon groups) trombone swingers.

Another Ellington trombonist, Joe "Tricky Sam" Nanton, received much attention, mainly for his "jungle music" wa-wa sounds on numerous Ellington pieces. His distinctive horn was a kind of trademark feature of the Duke's band from 1926 until 1948, when Tricky Sam died.

Nanton made the trombone talk. And Vic Dickenson made it loquacious and more articulate. Dickenson became even better known after the Swing Era, and was one of the fierce individualists of jazz. His playing demonstrated fire, invention, wit, and certainly a language of its own. A reader must hear him play only—on recordings now, and some of his best recorded work was with Bobby Hackett—to comprehend why so many found his personal approach to jazz trombone absolutely delightful.

Lou McGarity, a handsome Irishman from Georgia, described as only "capable" in a major jazz encyclopedia, was another great Swing Era player, light years beyond merely capable. He joined Goodman in 1940, after working for non-swinger Ben Bernie, and immediately won rave notices from all with musical ears. Aside from the superb Urbie Green, who was with Goodman long after the Swing Era, McGarity was no doubt the greatest jazz trombone player ever in a Goodman band for any substantial period.

Tommy Dorsey, only a so-so jazz player, was a master of the ballad, with a full, gorgeous sound few could match. Georg Brunis (originally George Brunies) went to Chicago from New Orleans with the New Orleans Rhythm Kings in 1919, and during the Swing Era was a key member of Muggsy Spanier's Ragtime Band. He was a vigorous player and quite a comic and singer, too, famed for his rendition of *Sister Kate,* the shimmy expert. Bandleader Will Bradley, trombonist Glenn Miller's favorite trombonist, was certainly an accomplished player. Cutty Cutshall, McGarity's teammate in the Goodman band when McGarity got almost every trombone solo, came into his own in the 1940s in small bands, proving to be a blisteringly hot player with a Butterfield group at Nick's and with similar devout truth-players at Eddie Condon's club.

Toward the end of the Swing Era, previously extolled Bill Harris was raising trombone fire to blazing heights with Woody Herman's "First Herd." His style, or whatever it was, was singular and marvelous, ranging from savage and raucous shouts to warm, soft purrs. If jazz is the sound of surprise, as Whitney Balliett suggested, and surely in some ways it is, one of the best examples ever is how Bill Harris played the trombone.

Many Distinctive Clarinetists

The clarinet has not been a major instrument in jazz for many years now, perhaps because it is a difficult instrument to play well, much harder, for example, than the ever-popular tenor saxophone.

But it was certainly still a major jazz instrument during the Swing Era and the most famous, most applauded player of the period was a clarinetist, Benny Goodman. As the Swing Era's central figure, there has been much about Goodman in this book already, but a few more paragraphs here:

As even those who find reason to knock Goodman admit, he had great technical command of his instrument. But his artistry went much further than that. His "hot" playing was inspired, characterized by a careful, constant concern for dynamic shadings sometimes described as "heart." He had a fine tone in the upper register as well as in the lower, easier-to-play register, known as chalumeau. His personal approach to improvisation combined great rhythmic drive and—as clarinetist Bob Wilber has written—"a concept of the instrument that was so musical, almost like a singer's voice." Wilber also accurately wrote about Goodman: "He played with incredible ease on an instrument that is extremely difficult to play in a free relaxed way, but it was done so effortlessly that he made it seem like the easiest thing in the world … it was so natural, with never a feeling of technique for technique's sake."

Though probably best known for dazzling runs and arpeggios played with assurance and brio on rapid tempos, he could—in the words of clarinetist Ed Hall—"play a slow tune note-by-note and still make it jazz." Goodman habitually treated lovely melodies with care, restraint, and passion. He also had the habit, particularly noticeable on his small group work, of leading the next soloist in with a brief introductory phrase, as if to give him a note to begin on. He did not leave the next soloist hanging on a clarinet high note. Even Leonard Feather, the veteran critic who was enormously enthusiastic about Buddy DeFranco's non-Goodmanesque clarinet playing during the bop period, wrote in his 1957 *The Book of Jazz:* "the extraordinary musicianship of Goodman made further progress on the instrument a challenge almost impossible to meet. By the late 1940s, when there were hundreds of able saxophonists and trumpeters embellishing the jazz stage, the number of comparatively gifted clarinetists could be counted on the rings of one instrument."

Perhaps it goes even further than that. There are some, including this writer, who believe that Goodman's extraordinary clarinet playing made every other style of jazz clarinet, during the Swing Era and ever since, seem somewhat limited or somewhat mechanical. Even today, clarinetists who play in a Goodmanesque way seem to be hotter, more convincing jazz players.

"Benny stories," reporting how unsophisticated, gauche, goofy, and preoccupied with music the man could be, were a part of jazz lore during and after the Swing Era. His inability to remember names (not tunes or chord progressions) even when on stage, was frequently noted. "Benny stories" were told with glee and sometimes vexation by his sidemen, but he could be jolly and fun when all was going well musically. And he was secretly generous to musicians down on their luck.

He loved to practice and did not understand why others did not. Morning band practice was not unusual, only part of the price a musician paid working for Benny during the Swing Era. (When I saw him in his room one afternoon at the Carlton Hotel in Washington after the Swing Era had ended, upon my arrival he was, typically, practicing clarinet. Mozart. He was not playing Mozart with his band that evening.) Goodman submitted to interviews but seldom enjoyed them. He did not like to talk about music with people he believed did not know much about music. Unlike, say, Woody Herman, a popular interviewee known for his hip wit and a desire and natural ability to win reporters over, Goodman was often not comfortable answering press questions, and his usually curt answers suggested a wary edginess.

During the Swing Era, Goodman's clarinet frequently moved into gutty sounds that were seldom found in his solos after he switched from single embouchure to double embouchure for a purer, more "classical" sound. This was in the 1950s when he studied with Reginald Kell and became more involved with formal music. Many believe that Goodman lost some of his "hotness" when he switched embouchures (with the mouthpiece held between both lips instead of the upper lip and lower teeth). Still, as many of his post–Swing Era recordings prove, he was occasionally as hot as ever and he remained an exciting jazz player until his death at age seventy-seven in 1986. Goodman was found with clarinet in hand after suffering from a fatal heart attack. He had been playing a piece by Mozart.

By 1938 Artie Shaw was nearly as famous as Goodman. This was partly due to Shaw's best-selling record of *Begin the Beguine* (certainly not one of Cole Porter's best songs), the kind of number-one smash-hit record that Goodman never had. Shaw had a marvelous clarinet sound, full and certain in the instrument's challenging upper register, and a graceful, lyrical approach to improvisation. Although Shaw's solos seemed more "set" or mentally prearranged than Goodman's, Shaw was a commanding soloist, distinctively different and definitely no imitator or emulator of Goodman.

Shaw was known for grumbling about the music business, and jitterbugs too, but he had a huge following. Much handsomer than Goodman (or most men for that matter) and well known as a ladies man (he dated Betty Grable long before she became Mrs. Harry James), Shaw's marriages made him a household name even in households where no one knew or cared about his top-drawer musicianship. His most famous wives were movie star Lana Turner (his third marriage, her first, when she was "The Sweater Girl," a marriage that lasted four months), Jerome Kern's lovely daughter Betty Kern, movie star Ava Gardner, *Forever Amber* novelist Kathleen Winsor, Broadway actress Doris Dowling, and still another movie star, Evelyn Keyes, to whom Shaw was wed much longer than any of the others. Goodman was no competition to Shaw in this area of activity. Goodman married only once. His wife was John Hammond's divorced sister Alice. This 1942 marriage startled many because Alice came from a family of great wealth and social position and had been married, in 1927, to a member of the British Parliament. Goodman's background, in contrast, included an impoverished childhood in a Chicago Jewish ghetto. There was nothing subtle about their obvious class differences, and he was decidedly not viewed as Social Register material. But according to those who knew them best, it was a happy marriage until a heart attack caused her death in 1978.

Unlike Goodman, Shaw always viewed himself as an intellectual, and when compared to some prominent jazz musicians who could be mentioned here, he was. But as his 1952 book *The Trouble With Cinderella* suggests, Shaw was not a major league intellectual although he was major league all the way in jazz.

Shaw led excellent bands, notably one in the early forties that included such splendid sidemen as Johnny Guarnieri, Billy Butterfield, Hot Lips Page, Les Robinson, and Jack Jenney. (Butterfield and Jenney are featured on Shaw's deservedly famous recording of *Star Dust*.) And Shaw's Gramercy Five small group recordings with pianist Guarnieri (sometimes on harpsichord) and trumpet player Butterfield using a mute were delightful, charming, superb. Shaw stopped playing the clarinet in public, and reportedly even in private, decades ago.

Among other distinctively different Swing Era clarinetists, Edmond Hall was one of the most exciting. His favorite clarinetist was Goodman, but he didn't try to play like Goodman at all and why should he? He could play like Edmond Hall and no one else could do that. Hall had a fiery, reedy sound, plus an obvious ability to swing as mightily as anyone. (An ability to swing is something that some have and some don't and it cannot be taught.)

One of jazz history's great clarinetists, Jimmie Noone, was not making big money like Goodman and Shaw, but he was still thrilling music lovers during the Swing Era in Chicago clubs. And one of his admirers, Joe Marsala, continued the warm Noone approach to clarinet in New York clubs.

Buster Bailey, who had sometimes played duets with Goodman (who was seven years younger than Bailey) when both studied clarinet with Franz Schoepp in Chicago, was highly skilled. He might have become a classical player rather than a jazz player (with Henderson's band in the 1920s and with John Kirby's popular small group during the Swing Era) if racial prejudice in the halls of symphonic beauty had not made that impossible.

The extremely overweight Irving Prestopnik, known to one and all as Fazola (as in do-re-mi-*fa-so-la,* because as a kid in New Orleans he could read music and his musical colleagues at that time could not), won the hearts of jazz fans with his gorgeous clarinet sound in the Bob Crosby band. A heavy drinker, he died at age thirty-six in 1949.

Another accomplished drinker, Charles Ellsworth "Pee Wee" Russell, was a major hero for jazz lovers who liked their music straight, not watered down in any way with written or even "head" arrangements. Pee Wee, light in weight but not a peewee in stature, with an expressive countenance that made him a "photo op" before that term came into the language, had a passionate fan club mainly composed of traditional and/or Dixieland jazz enthusiasts. And these club, or cult, members were quick to stress, rightfully, the obvious honesty of his clarinet playing, which was so dramatically unlike the clarinet playing of anyone else, living, dead, or yet to be.

Set solos were not in his bag. Indeed, every Pee Wee solo seemed like an angst-loaded struggle. He habitually encountered uncharted, challenging melodic twists and turns as he went along, as if in combat with his instrument. The listener, usually entranced and sometimes spellbound, struggled with him, rooting that the lovable Pee Wee would somehow get through his self-imposed improvisatory trials and tribulations okay, which he customarily did, creating amazement and bringing joy to the world of those who came to Nick's and other New York clubs to hear the one, the only Pee Wee, lightweight champion of heavyweight jazz truth! Pee Wee may not have battled the bottle as often as those who loved him wished, but he always battled the clarinet and usually won by knockout. His so-called "funny notes" sometimes encapsulated the very spirit of jazz.

When Russell first achieved national attention, but not the good money that can go with it, Pee Wee was famous for his "dirty tone" as well as for the growls, squeaks, squawks, and wavering notes he forced out of his clarinet. Goodman once said he thought too much air was escaping from Pee Wee's lips as he played. But however his dirty tone was created, and I always suspected it was due in part to Pee Wee's second-rate instrument (held together with rubber bands, according to his great admirer George Frazier), it surely helped to make his playing distinctive, and cherished by some who sneered at more graceful and technically able jazz clarinetists such as Goodman, Shaw, Johnny Mince, Jimmy Hamilton, and Hank D'Amico. Some Pee Wee admirers were comfortable calling such players "glib" in contrast to Pee Wee. And Pee Wee, to be sure, was never glib.

I was one Pee Wee admirer who thought he played much better at age sixty than he did when I first heard him at Nick's in the Village during the Swing Era. In any event, by 1966, a few years before his death at almost sixty-three, his famous dirty tone was decidedly not so dirty, and I asked him about it.

"Oh, yes, that dirty tone ... why is it that people like to tag you with something like that?" Pee Wee laughed in his somewhat shy but deep voice, "I never sought a dirty tone and I never considered myself a Dixieland clarinet player," he told me.

Certainly one reason he sounded better then, long after the Swing Era, was his instrument, a fine Buffet. At that time, too, more and more people were finally beginning to realize that Pee Wee was not just a Dixieland clarinet player.

Humble by nature, quick to rap his own work and praise other musicians, including Goodman, he was more popular than ever in his later years. So, Pee Wee may not have been a great clarinetist, but he was a great jazz artist. His improvisations were often ingenious, usually compelling, and customarily heartfelt. He was inimitable and his playing reached people in a meaningful way.

Ellingtonians, including Ellington himself, continually praised Barney Bigard, also one of the easiest of all clarinet players for jazz history students to identify on a recording. But he was not a hot player and his solos did not involve what is generally considered jazz excitement. His playing was distinguished by a gorgeous tone in the chalumeau register, frequent chromatic runs, and glissandi galore. With Ellington's orchestra from 1928 until 1942, his clarinet is prominent on dozens of Ellington pieces including *Mood Indigo*, which he helped to write. He also made some remarkable Bluebird recordings with small Ellington groups around 1940 including *Charlie the Chulo* and *Lament for Javanette*, which demonstate Bigard's sensuous sound extremely well. Perhaps striptease dancers somewhere have used *Javanette* as music to strip by, and if none ever has, they should.

Like other New Orleans clarinetists including Johnny Dodds, Sidney Bechet, Omer Simeon, and Edmond Hall, Bigard played the Albert system, not the newer Boehm system used by Goodman and most all of his contemporaries. Jimmy Dorsey, a notable exception because he played an Albert clarinet, was an able clarinetist though more widely known for his alto saxophone playing.

Other standout clarinetists of the Swing Era included Hank D'Amico (with Red Norvo and others), Johnny Mince (with Tommy Dorsey), Peanuts Hucko (then beginning to sound more and more like Goodman), Abe Most (with Les Brown), Mahlon Clark (with Ray McKinley), and Jimmy Hamilton (who joined Ellington in 1942, well described by Leonard Feather as one who "might be called a low-blood-pressure Goodman").

As for Woody Herman, he will be remembered more as a major bandleader and appealing singer than as a clarinetist—as an intelligent, witty, extremely nice guy, too.

In the late 1930s, teenager Buddy DeFranco proved he had mastered the tricky mechanics of the clarinet during jam sessions at Billy Krechmer's in his hometown, Philadelphia. And although he was on the road with Gene Krupa's band by 1942, DeFranco's fame came after the Swing Era had more or less ended, when echoes of Bird were heard in his work after bop Dizzily oo-bop-sha-bammed in.

Lester Was Different

Unlike the clarinet, the tenor saxophone was not a major jazz instrument in the 1920s, but it certainly was just that during the Swing Era. And though many admirers of Coleman Hawkins may strongly disagree, to my mind *the* tenor saxophonist of the Swing Era was Lester Young.

Numerous jazz essays have suggested that Young was under-appreciated during the Swing Era. That's not the way I remember it. In my circle of jazz fanatics, and in many similar circles I'm sure, it was Lester this and Lester that, every recorded Lester solo was played and replayed, and Lester was a major reason not to miss Basie or, later, to visit Fifty-second Street. For many of us, every chance to hear Lester Young play was an event that had to be made.

Lester Young, nicknamed "Pres" (for President) by his friend Billie Holiday, created melodies to remember with ease, his tenor saxophone was not overblown as was fashionable then, he avoided sensation, and before the war his tone was lovely, if softer than most. And could he swing! His best recordings remain absolutely timeless. In addition to his many solos with the original Basie band, even more impressive are his records with Basie small groups (*Lester Leaps In, Lester Leaps Again, After Theater Jump,* for example), briefer but classic solos with Teddy Wilson groups featuring vocals by Billie Holiday, with Nat Cole *(Indiana, I Can't Get Started),* and with Johnny Guarnieri, Slam Stewart, and Sid Catlett *(Sometimes I'm Happy, Just You, Just Me)*. Anyone who has an urge to recall or discover the best music of the Swing Era would be wise to include these recordings on a must-hear list.

Those who keep writing that Lester was some kind of bop "precursor" have it all wrong. Bop harmonics, bop licks and tricks were never in his bag. As he said when bop was most popular: "Don't call me a bop musician. If you have to call me something, call me a *swing* musician."

At a time when Coleman Hawkins was considered the yardstick of tenor sax playing, Lester Young came up with something that was not only different but blissfully and relentlessly melodic. Perhaps his music was less obviously emotional than that of most tenor soloists, but his fire was always apparent, never banked. His solos never yelled. They hummed, flowingly, in a relaxed and reflective way.

93

Lester Young was an unusual man who distrusted most "ofays," affected curious haircuts, and was known to mumble "bells, man, ding, dong" to clubowners and hangers-on. Also, as happened to some other great Swing Era players, his heavy drinking caught up with him. But he certainly brought countless hours of musical pleasure to the most musically aware, and there is much reason to consider him one of the three most influential musicians in jazz history (the other two being Louis Armstrong and Charlie Parker). I am thankful that I wasn't born too late, that I heard Lester in his prime, during the Swing Era, when he could really play.

Much has been written about Lester's "horizontal" approach to improvisation in contrast to the "vertical" approach of Coleman Hawkins, suggesting that Hawkins was primarily involved with running chords, thus up and down on the music manuscript, not forward, horizontally. But Hawkins did much more than merely run chords, by rote, bright harmonic thinking, whatever, and it is best to leave all this to those deep thinkers in the jazz criticism field who persist in the idea that jazz is a problem that must be solved and somehow explained in print.

Lester Young influenced—inspired might be the more accurate word—countless tenor saxophone players including such exceptional ones as Stan Getz and Zoot Sims and many not so famous. Alto saxophone players, too, including Paul Desmond, whose great playing certainly helped to make pianist Dave Brubeck financially successful. You can hear Lester in other jazz instruments, too, in Charlie Christian's guitar, for example, and even in the playing of the great jazz harmonica player "Toots" Thielemans.

As for Hawkins, although Antoine (Adolphe) Sax invented the tenor saxophone, it was Coleman Hawkins who made it a *musical* instrument. It is sometimes forgotten that until the Hawk came along the tenor sax was considered a kind of joke instrument, to be used for moaning, cackling, squealing, grunting, and other not-quite-musical sound effects.

In the early 1920s, Hawkins used a staccato, slap-tongue technique that made him wince in later years when he listened to his early recordings with Fletcher Henderson's orchestra. By 1929, however, the basic Hawkins style had evolved, as Henderson's *Teapot Dome Blues* suggests. The tenor sax champion went to England in 1934 after discovering he had many fans there, and after being viewed properly as jazz royalty for five years in Europe, he returned to the States in 1939 at the height of the Swing Era. That year he made his famous Bluebird recording of *Body and Soul*, a three-minute classic available for thirty-five cents. Teddy Wilson told me he thought this was "about as perfect a jazz performance as is possible." Many agree.

The very sound of the Hawkins tenor saxophone, muscular and virile, was imitated and emulated by countless players, but most lacked his great musical ingenuity, precision, and originality. Watching the Hawk, in his customary double-breasted suit, play chorus after chorus of a lovely old standard, with each chorus remarkably different, is a cherished memory for this writer.

Aside from Lester Young, chubby, jolly Leon "Chu" Berry was probably the main tenor sax rival of Hawkins for the hearts of the swing-convinced. Chu was a great player—listen to those records he made with Roy Eldridge on Commodore!—and is curiously all but forgotten in some jazz history books.

Bud Freeman, the best player of the Austin High School "gang" from Chicago, did not play like Hawkins or anybody else. He always had a style of his own, and although there will be no attempt to explain his way of playing jazz here, the reader is advised to imagine how a jazz clarinet solo might sound on tenor sax and this might put you in the right ballpark. Eddie Miller, a major soloist in Bob Crosby's band, was somewhat similar to Freeman, but had his own softer, more restrained, and irrepressibly melodic approach. Both Freeman and Miller were often pigeonholed as Dixieland players, but such classification only proved that the pigeonholers categorized these two fine players by the company they kept and not by listening to how they played.

Ben Webster began as an able follower of Hawkins but became distinctively one-of-a-kind, namely Ben Webster. A man with broad shoulders and a straight back, he was called "Big Ben" and sometimes "The Brute," but there was nothing brutish about the way he played a ballad. He was tender, not brutish, and romantic, not gruff. His artistry was one of the more exquisite examples of delicacy combined with virility to be found in twentieth-century music. His solos with the Ellington band from 1939–1943, ranging from the jumping *Cottontail* to the lovely *All Too Soon*, are as compelling today as they were then. His post–Swing Era playing seemed even better. As he became older, his tone sounded larger and warmer, his concern for proper notes in proper places more habitual. He had a way of adding a slight embellishment here, a trickle of a completely new melody there, a smear of surprise when least expected, all presented with a persistent singing quality. Some have described Webster's playing as erotic. Maybe so. And if so, it is surely splendid eroticism as well as splendid jazz music.

Hodges, Carter, Smith

During the Swing Era, before Charlie Parker and bop, jazz solos on the E-flat alto saxophone were not nearly as plentiful as those on the B-flat tenor saxophone. Alto sax solos were seldom heard in bands led by Goodman, Tommy Dorsey, Miller, Herman, and many others. Of course alto saxophone solos were good and plenty in the Jimmy Dorsey band because Jimmy played alto. And yes, lead alto player Earle Warren, and later Tab Smith, had occasional solos with the Basie band although tenor saxophone soloists dominated. But three of the Swing Era's greatest musicians were alto saxophone players and major soloists: Johnny Hodges, Benny Carter, and Willie Smith.

Hodges joined Ellington at age twenty-one in 1928 and by the late 1930s was probably the most admired of all Ellington musicians. Charlie Barnet said this about the man nicknamed "Rabbit," a master of the blues and the ballad, and indeed just about any other music used as a basis for jazz playing: "There has never been anybody like Johnny and never a successful imitator. There was no [Hodges] school like there was with Charlie Parker, because nobody had the tone and the soul Johnny had, and so they couldn't do what he did."

Probably best known for his compelling, lovely, commanding glissandi-loaded solos on slower pieces such as *I Got It Bad* or *Passion Flower*, Hodges swung delightfully and distinctively on bouncier tempos, as is easily proven by dozens of his recordings with Ellington, Teddy Wilson small groups, and his own combos.

Benny Carter was the other most admired alto sax player of the Swing Era. Carter swung mightily in a somewhat dignified, restrained way and was always clearly the master of his instrument and whatever song he was playing. Those who believe jazz must involve *melodic* improvisation need look no further than Carter. Almost entirely self-taught, he played other instruments as well, including trumpet, and was also a major arranger of music.

Between sets one night before World War II, as the Carter band played on a boat cruising down the Potomac River, Carter played solo piano, for kicks apparently. And he did not play the piano the way many arrangers do, stressing chords, not melody. He had a most active right hand. After he had finished, I was chatting with the trombone soloist in his band, and said: "Gee, I didn't know Benny could play the piano that well!" The excellent trombonist replied: "Oh yes, he plays just about every instrument well. He plays the trombone better than I do."

Another highly praised alto man of the Swing Era was the leader of the Jimmie Lunceford reed section, Willie Smith, a remarkable soloist as well. He swung gracefully with a fine tone and a cheerful, melodic approach. He was as inimitable as Hodges or Carter, still another example of the infinite variety of Swing Era stylists.

The most widely known alto saxophone player in America, Jimmy Dorsey, was a most capable jazz player, too. Born in 1904, he was popular with jazz fans long before the Swing Era because of his recordings with Red Nichols and others during the 1920s. Lester Young was one of his many young admirers. Jimmy also proved that being a nice guy did not interfere with leading a popular big band.

Hilton Jefferson, older than Dorsey and a veteran big band player by the time the Swing Era began, was with Chick Webb and Cab Calloway during those swinging years and was another alto player held in high esteem. Like some other standout Swing Era players not well known to the general public, by 1954—with bop dominating the jazz scene, most big bands a memory, and rock or something like it capturing teenagers and the record industry—Jefferson had trouble finding enough work to remain in music regularly and became a bank guard. About that time, when explaining to me how bad the jazz situation was in New York, Roy Eldridge stressed Jefferson's position as a bank guard, which Eldridge said summed it all up.

Accomplished lead alto players who seldom soloed were important players during the Swing Era and among the best were Hymie Schertzer (with Goodman and Tommy Dorsey) and Les Robinson (with Goodman and Shaw).

The baritone saxophone, an octave lower than the alto, did not become a fashionable solo instrument in jazz until the Swing Era was about over, with Ernie Caceres, Serge Chaloff, Pepper Adams, and, most notably, Gerry Mulligan leading the way. During the Swing Era, it was considered too inflexible to be a solo instrument, despite Harry Carney, certainly *the* baritone saxophone player of the era. Carney's baritone in Ellington's band was, for forty-five years, the big bottom sound in the Duke's lush harmonic world. And during the Swing

Era, Carney, almost alone, was able to tame this instrument for jazz solos.

As Harry Carney was another way of saying baritone saxophone, Sidney Bechet was another way of saying soprano saxophone. Born in 1897, Bechet had played with the Eagle Band of New Orleans around 1912 as a clarinetist, but during the early 1920s fell in love with the soprano. His compulsion to swing never diminished, and his wide vibrato and fine intonation, on an instrument said to be difficult to keep in proper pitch, was considered matchless. Tenor and alto saxophonist Charlie Barnet also played soprano well, as did a few others, but former clarinetist Bechet, who could not read music, was numero uno on his instrument of choice. Young Bob Wilber studied with Bechet in the mid-1940s and certainly became proficient on the instrument, often sounding much like Bechet, but eventually switched to clarinet, with an obvious Goodmanesque style.

A Dozen Great Drummers

In the beginning was the drum. Boomlay, boomlay, boomlay, BOOM, and the drummer was an important player in Swing Era jazz. Also, mainly because of Gene Krupa, even drum solos became popular.

Then, as now, good drummers were hard to find. Rare was and is still a proper adjective for drummers who can keep steady time, have an ear for the dynamics of music, who are sensitive to what the other musicians in the band are trying to play, and who can spark a band by giving it rhythmic push and wallop. Drumming isn't easy. It only looks easy, and the idea that "anyone can keep time" is nonsense.

Among the greatest of the Swing Era drummers were Big Sid Catlett, Jo Jones, and Dave Tough. And these men had the ability, and good taste, to alter their drumming style to fit the kind of music being played.

Catlett, who died in 1951 at the age of forty-one, could rock a big band as few could, or soften down so much that a listener would be conscious only of the beat and forget there was even a drummer on the bandstand, which was precisely what happened to me one night on Fifty-second Street when Big Sid, using wire brushes ever so softly, was one-third of a pianist's trio. And it would take a drummer to explain how Catlett was able to get such a distinctive sound from his cymbals, if anyone could.

Jones was the complete master of his instrument. And, as someone asked, what other drummer could solo with his eyebrows? Jones got a clean, not mushy, sound with his brushes, and did wonders with the high hat cymbal. The word impeccable is overused, but Jo's rhythmic time was certainly impeccable. When he was a key member of the first Basie band, other drummers received more national attention—the highly skilled and charismatic Krupa, who got such a great sound from his snare, and the most able Ray McKinley, for example—but Jones always had the rapt attention of other drummers. And he was a rhythm-section man first and foremost—not a flashy soloist—lighting the fire with guitarist Freddie Green, bass player Walter Page, and pianist Basie that enabled the first Basie band and its remarkable soloists to swing as perhaps no band has ever swung so consistently. Jones is credited with moving the major time-keeping tool from bass drum to cymbal.

Dave Tough also always played for the band, not for the crowd. As a youngster he was a standout with Chicagoans playing what some would call a kind of Dixieland, and during the Swing Era he kept the beat where it was supposed to be with the big bands of Tommy Dorsey and Benny Goodman, then became a rhythmic dynamo in Woody Herman's "First Herd." He followed Krupa in the Goodman band and this was quite a change in Benny's band. Tough was never sensational like Krupa, did not like to solo and rarely did, and was a much quieter drummer than the popular Krupa. With Herman, Tough was something else again. It was hard for this writer to believe that the loud drummer whipping the "First Herd" into rhythmic splendor was the same man who usually kept his volume way down with Goodman (*Scarecrow* being a notable exception to this generality). Tough was always a musician's musician, never widely known to the general public as Krupa was. When Tough died at age forty in 1948, after fracturing his skull falling down in a Newark street, an Associated Press obituary writer obviously had no idea who he was, thus the sentence "his wife said he had played with Tommy Dorsey, Benny Goodman, and Woody Herman." As he had, beautifully. Tough was known as a wit and intellectual, for reason, and as a heavy drinker, too, also for reason.

Gallant Chick Webb, a little hunchback with a tubercular spine whose band was enormously popular at the Savoy Ballroom, was a master of the bass drum and cymbals, too. He was an inspired, powerhouse player, adored by Gene Krupa and many other first-rate drummers of the Swing Era. Webb died of tuberculosis in 1939, at age thirty-seven. A large funeral followed in Baltimore. His young singer, Ella Fitzgerald, sang *My Buddy* beside his casket as musicians and fans wept. Like most others who saw his band, to me Webb remains unforgettable.

Among other most memorable drummers of the era: Cozy Cole, the phenomenally fast-with-the-sticks Buddy Rich (whose *Quiet Please* feature with Tommy Dorsey's band was definitely not quiet), veterans Baby Dodds ("I don't use brushes") and Zutty Singleton, George Wettling, and J. C. Heard.

Years after the Swing Era had ended, J. C. Heard, while listening to some records at my home, was asked to name his favorite drummer. I had expected him to name Jo Jones or Chick Webb, knowing he admired both of these men. But his answer was immediate and firm: "Buddy Rich! He has two hands, two feet, and a mind!"

As for those who believed that both Rich and Krupa played too loudly, they never heard another prominent big band drummer, Cliff Leeman, punish the cymbals and other drum paraphernalia with Charlie Barnet's band. Leeman was certainly the loudest good drummer I ever heard (loud bad drummers were not uncommon, then as now, but they don't count). Leeman did, however, seem to bring his volume down considerably when he later played with Eddie Condon small groups. Perhaps Barnet encouraged Leeman to play as loudly as possible, I don't know.

The string bass (bass violin or "bull fiddle") was an essential instrument for every jazz band, large or small, during the Swing Era, a wise and understandable replacement for the tuba. But it was used only as the harmonic bottom of the rhythm section and was not considered, as it is today, a melodic solo instrument as well. That is, not until Jimmy Blanton. This young man, with Ellington from 1939 until his death due to tuberculosis at age twenty-one in 1942, proved eloquently that the bass could do much more than handle four notes to the bar. He made sixteenths sound natural on bass and opened the way for a fistful of superb bass players in the 1950s and beyond. Before Blanton, bass solos were rare.

Among the best of the Swing Era bassists: Milt Hinton (with Calloway then and still playing beautifully as an octogenarian at this writing), Artie Bernstein (with Goodman), Bobby Haggart (whose duet with Bob Crosby teammate drummer Ray Bauduc, *Big Noise From Winnetka,* was a surprise best-selling record), Walter Page (with

Basie), and Slam Stewart (who created novel and humorous solos by simultaneously bowing the bass and hum-grunting an octave apart from the notes being played by his left hand).

Guitar: Acoustic Rhythm Instrument

Despite the marvelous and revolutionary amplified guitar single-string solos of Charlie Christian with the Goodman sextet from late 1939 until 1941, the guitar was primarily an unamplified rhythm instrument during the Swing Era.

A rhythm section was considered woefully weak and incomplete without the sound and bite of the acoustic f-hole guitar. This non-electric instrument served to tie the drums and bass together into a rhythmic force. An amplified or electric guitar simply cannot do this well at all because it is not as crisp, the sound is fuzzier, buzzier, mushier, and naturally more electronic. For some who remember the Swing Era, a rhythm section without the unamplified guitar stroke is not a true rhythm section. Count Basie maintained the Swing Era rhythm-section sound for decades after the era was long gone, with Freddie Green (who joined Basie in 1937) still in his guitar chair until Basie's death in 1984 (and in fact Freddie was still with the Countless Basie band at the time of his own death in 1987 when he was almost seventy-six).

Green became the best known of all rhythm guitarists because of his great if often taken-for-granted artistry and his decades with Basie. But there were many other fine rhythm guitarists active during the Swing Era. These included George Van Eps, who became an amazing soloist, using chords as well as single strings, and a standout Van Eps student, Allan Reuss. Reuss was one of the most important players in the first Goodman band. Among other top-rank Swing Era rhythm men: Carmen Mastren (with Tommy Dorsey), Benny Heller (Goodman and James), Mike Bryan (Goodman and Shaw), the veteran Carl Kress (with Whiteman during the 1920s, with many top small groups during the Swing Era), Tommy Morgan (Goodman and Shaw), and Steve Jordan (Bradley, Shaw, Teddy Powell, Bob Chester, Freddie Slack, Boyd Raeburn, Stan Kenton, and Goodman later in the 1950s).

Good rhythm players have been hard to find for many years now because jazz guitarists concentrate on amplified solo work, and as Jordan said, "few of them know how to voice chords properly and there is no demand that they learn how."

It was a young man, dead by twenty-three, who almost single-handedly made amplified solo guitar a major new voice in jazz. And Charlie Christian was, as John Hammond said, "one of the great natural musicians in jazz history."

Responsible for getting Christian his opportunity with Goodman, and thus his fame, Hammond heard Christian in Oklahoma City and was convinced he belonged in the Goodman small group. He called Benny, then in California, and told him: "I've just heard the greatest guitar player since Eddie Lang. He plays electric guitar and—"

"Who the hell wants to hear an electric-guitar player?" Benny interrupted.

As is well known, Goodman did hear Christian, who knocked him out, and the world of jazz guitar soon changed.

There have been many Christian-inspired players—notably such onward Christian soldiers as Barney Kessel, Oscar Moore, Herb Ellis, and Tal Farlow—but Christian remains one-of-a-kind. Unlike most amplified guitar soloists heard today who can't seem to play too many notes, Christian sounded more like a saxophone player playing guitar than a guitarist, complete with a saxophonist's breathing holes, or gulps of air. He phrased like a saxophonist and his melodic improvisations were uncluttered by needless notes and runs, appropriate for one inspired by Lester Young.

Christian's recordings with the Goodman sextet are classics, and he was even better on the bandstand because his solos were longer. I well remember that Benny didn't hesitate to let Charlie play chorus after chorus on occasion. The Goodman sextet, in person, had no three-minute time restriction for each tune as it did in a recording studio.

Just as Christian and many other Swing Era musicians and enthusiasts knew some Lester Young solos by heart, many of us knew Charlie Christian's solos by heart, too. He was one of the marvels of the Swing Era.

Some jazz authorities keep describing Christian as a "precursor of bop." Beware of that idea. Certainly the recordings that a fan made of Christian's playing at Minton's in Harlem, a breeding place for what became known as be-bop, then bop, proves no such thing, as they contend. And who knows if his playing might have changed and become boppier? If some other popular swing players had died when Christian did, perhaps they too would now be

102

part of the bop-precursor list developed by those who view jazz through bop-tinted glasses.

Another guitar marvel, and one who was a real acoustic player, meaning he played loudly and certainly needed no amp to be heard, was the Belgian gypsy Django Reinhardt. Americans knew his work only by recordings then, unless they traveled to Paris. He recorded with prominent American jazz players in France and he and violinist Stéphane Grappelli (then spelled Grappelly) created music that swung in the Quintet of the Hot Club of France. Reinhardt did not appear in the United States until 1946 and by this time he was, curiously, using an electric guitar. Who knows why?

Reinhardt was an utterly fantastic player with amazing pick technique although two of his fingers on his left hand (his fingerboard hand) were immobilized. He used these fingers to "deaden" strings for octave work but he couldn't use them to get a note of music. In 1928, he was an eighteen-year-old violinist who also played guitar and banjo when his gypsy *roulotte* (wagon), camped near Paris, caught fire. Django was so badly burned that doctors told him his left arm would have to be amputated. He protested, hysterically, and was left with a functional arm although the use of two fingers was gone. He soon discovered that his violin playing was a caricature of what it had been before the fire but found he could still play the guitar, though much differently than he had before.

Guitarists regarded Reinhardt with awe. Today, one of his pieces, *Nuages,* is still played, reverently, by top guitarists. Django could not read music (nor could Christian), but so what? His playing had bite, power, ingenuity, great and rhythmically precise speed, and a touch of melancholy, too. He was only forty-three years old when he died in 1953.

Of all the non-American jazz players, Reinhardt is probably the finest ever—also the most distinctively un-American. Unlike most every other foreign jazz player, he did not imitate or emulate any American jazz player. He played his own way. And his way was inimitable.

And there were great Swing Era players on other instruments. Who can recall those years without remembering Lionel Hampton, Red Norvo, Joe Venuti, and Stuff Smith?

Has anyone ever swung harder on the violin than Venuti? Well, maybe one who was certainly not a polished violinist like Venuti, namely Hezekiah Leroy Gordon "Stuff" Smith. By 1936, with an

November 18, 1946

DOWN BEAT

DJANGO REINHARDT

MUSIC NEWS FROM COAST-TO-COAST

25 CENTS
FOREIGN 30¢

$5 PER YEAR

Django the Great—Belgian gypsy Django Reinhardt, shown on the November 18, 1946, Down Beat *cover, had artistry that musicians, especially guitarists, found incredible. (Reprinted with permission from* Down Beat *magazine.)*

amplifier attached to his fiddle at the Onyx on Fifty-second Street, Stuff was an early Swing Era hero.

As a young man, Stuff's musical hero was Armstrong, and he played the violin as if it were a trumpet. An upbeat, witty, delightful man who was a ball to be with, his way with a violin was astonishing though flawed from a technical point of view. His fingering was unorthodox and he did not use all of the bow, only about six or eight inches at the end of the bow. He said he liked to play "with plenty of drive," and so he did. His playing was an aural definition of what jazz music is all about.

Another Swing Era hero, another complete original with a seemingly unquenchable thirst to swing and swing and swing on chorus after chorus was Lionel Hampton, vibes champion. "Why stop now when we're really cooking and you ain't heard nothing yet" was Hamp's unstated but obvious mantra, one that could not be captured on the three-minute recordings of the time (the later long-playing records better served his inexhaustible energy and inventive musical mind).

Hampton, who began as a drummer, took what was considered a kind of joke instrument, the vibraphone or vibraharp, and made it not only a great *swinging* instrument for jazz but one that could be sensitive, delicate, and all such desirable warm things on a ballad (his first recording with Goodman was the lovely *Moonglow*). "Hamp" was a sensation with Goodman and, more than anyone else perhaps, inspired Benny to great heights of swinging abandon. Proof of this can be found on some of the everlastingly ripe Goodman quartet studio recordings, but more obviously on the radio hotel broadcasts, the 1937 and 1938 "airchecks" made by Bill Savory, later a Columbia recording engineer. For the quartet at its peerless best, and to hear just how Hampton could turn Benny and most everyone else on, listen to *Benny Sent Me* (it had no title when it was played on the bandstand), *Everybody Loves My Baby, I'm a Ding Dong Daddy From Dumas,* and others on the Columbia collection of these Goodman airchecks.

And before he left Goodman to organize his own big band in late 1940, Hampton made dozens of superb recordings (among a total of ninety-one) with pickup combos on Victor recordings for nearly five years. His "pickup" sidemen came from the bands of Goodman, Ellington, and Calloway and featured some of the Swing Era's finest players including Hodges, Hawkins, Webster, Williams, Chu Berry, Carter, Budd Johnson, and so many others, including the King Cole Trio before it was nationally famous. Anyone who seeks to catch the spirit of Swing Era music should listen to these Hampton records. As should anyone who believes it to be only a Big Band Era. Lionel Hampton was a phenomenal player and also one who stimulated other exceptional players easily, regularly, naturally.

Red Norvo, a master of the wooden, more-marimbalike xylophone, switched in 1943 to the metallic vibes with electric motor and sustaining pedal, thus adding vibrato. And his good taste, wit, finesse, gentleness, and musical ingenuity were well displayed in a 1945 Goodman sextet when Hampton was fronting his own successful big band.

There were other miscellaneous instruments, as *Down Beat* polls called them, put to good jazz use during the Swing Era. Joe Mooney's accordion was the key sound in his delightful 1946 quartet and later he made beautiful use of the organ on solo gigs. Mooney's keen ear for dynamics was a constant joy, as was his soft and hip singing. Yes, an argument can be made that musicians usually sing better than singers.

Major Pianists

There is, to be sure, another instrument yet to be discussed, an instrument whose jazz players reached new heights during the Swing Era: the piano, a major and incomparable instrument for so many kinds of music, including jazz, and one that should never be confused with the tinkling, toneless, dull, portable electronic instrument fashionable in some popular music circles today.

There were dozens of distinctively different Swing Era pianists. Some had developed exceptional skills a decade or more before the Swing Era, including ragtime pioneer Luckey Roberts, Willie "The Lion" Smith, and the father of Harlem's stride piano style, James P. Johnson, who inspired Fats Waller. (Roberts might be called stride piano's grandfather.) Ragtime veteran and composer Eubie Blake was around, too, although was not as nationally famous as he was to become decades later when he was one of the nation's most beloved truly senior citizens. Blake was one hundred years old when he died in 1983.

There was also Duke Ellington (his orchestra was by no means the only instrument he played with distinction) and many excellent younger players: Jess Stacy, Joe Sullivan, Clarence Profit, Herman Chittison, Mel Powell, Johnny Guarnieri, Joe Bushkin, Mary Lou Williams, Billy Kyle, Count Basie, Nat Cole, and so many others, including boogie-woogie "walking bass" specialists Meade Lux Lewis, Pete Johnson *(Roll 'Em, Pete!)*, and Albert Ammons.

But let's concentrate on five of the greatest, most famous, and most influential players of the Swing Era, each of whom brought

106

something new and exciting to jazz piano: Fats Waller, Earl Hines, Teddy Wilson, Art Tatum, and—as the Swing Era was ending—Erroll Garner.

Thomas "Fats" Waller was probably the most widely known jazz pianist during the Swing Era. Like Louis Armstrong, he was even popular with those who said they didn't like jazz much. This was because of his charisma, his inimitable singing, and his show business flair for fun and mugging that came through even on his recordings although such mugging could not be seen, only imagined.

Waller was a two-handed pianist if anyone ever was. His strong left hand, developed while studying how James P. Johnson did it, teamed with an accomplished right hand that rang treble notes with touch, tone, and assurance.

Waller's appetite for food, booze, and fun was enormous and what he brought to jazz and popular music was enormous, too. One who understood that life was to be enjoyed not endured, he was an entertainer in the best sense, as concerned with his audience as with his music. Fats was also a fast and gifted composer of popular music. He wrote dozens of delightful songs, many with lyrics by Andy Razaf such as *Ain't Misbehavin', Honeysuckle Rose, Keepin' Out of Mischief Now, Blue Turning Gray Over You,* and the stirring *Black and Blue.* (Razaf wrote words for many other composers, including Eubie Blake with whom he produced the jolly *You're Lucky to Me* and the haunting, plaintive *Memories of You,* the latter a challenge for any singer because of its wide melodic range.) Fats also wrote fine pieces for piano including the lovely *Jitterbug Waltz.*

This wit, comic, clown, and exceptional musician made hundreds of recordings, notably more than five hundred for Victor from 1934 until 1943 when he died at age thirty-nine. His recordings still prove what happiness, what joy, jazz can exude when it is played without pretension. Many of his recordings involved what musicians call "dog tunes," which were selected by the record company, not by Waller. In most cases, he had never played these songs before arriving at the recording studio. A look at the sheet music, a quick rehearsal, and that was it. Waller had a way of inspiring other players so that with Fats in charge everyone wanted to cook. Thus dog tunes came to life in the hands of Fats and his five musicians, notably guitarist Al Casey and tenor man Eugene "The Bear" Sedric. Fats could, and did, swing anything. He even turned Guy Lombardo's idiotic hit *Boo Hoo* into jazz music.

Earl Hines—known as "Fatha"—was the most influential of all jazz pianists during the late 1920s, largely because of his "Hot Five" records with Louis Armstrong. Teddy Wilson was only one of many fine young players who listened to those recorded solos by Hines closely and repeatedly. Leonard Feather wrote astutely about the emergence of Hines in his 1957 *The Book of Jazz:*

> He was often called "the trumpet style" pianist because the octaves on single note lines in the right hand, in contrast with the emphasis on chords that had predominated among the ragtimers and early stride pianists, lent the solos a bright and brassy quality that brought to mind the impact of a horn. Actually, Hines was much more than a pianist imitating a trumpeter, as the slogan falsely implied. He was essentially pianistic in his approach, in the sense that the left hand, far from playing a subsidiary role, was used more obliquely, with more diligence, taste, and technique than had ever been heard in jazz piano before.

Hines once said that he began to use octaves in his right hand simply to sound louder, to be heard over the brass, since he played without a microphone. In any event, Hines was always a full-bodied orchestral pianist and a vigorous swinger of enormous influence on other fine players during the Swing Era. His playing always had a wide dynamic range, startling runs, rhythmic drive. Any list of the greatest jazz musicians ever would be incomplete without the inclusion of Earl Hines. And he led one of the better swing bands, too.

Aside from Waller, probably the best known of all Swing Era jazz pianists was Teddy Wilson, largely because of his trio and quartet work with Goodman. Wilson was also a different kind of jazz pianist, more subdued than most, never flashy, with delicacy, precision, and elegance obvious, and with ingenious melodic improvisational ideas not so obvious. Wilson also had a true pianistic touch, which is not a characteristic of a surprisingly large number of able jazz pianists.

The biographer of Art Tatum, psychologist and pianist James Lester, spoke for many when he wrote this: "I loved Wilson's crisp and polished style, the clarity and sparkle of his melodic lines, the variety and interest of his left hand, the tenths constantly in motion, and those crystalline runs that sounded so spontaneous and yet inevitable at the same time."

In addition to his distinctive and highly influential piano playing, Wilson earned wide praise for his leadership of "all-star" small recording groups dating from 1935–1937, produced by John Hammond and featuring vocal choruses by Billie Holiday, usually. These now classic recordings also featured many of the Swing Era's finest players including members of the Basie, Goodman, and Ellington bands. Although Wilson had always been quick to praise Holiday's innate musicianship and inimitable sound on these records, he said years later that he would have preferred Ella Fitzgerald. But Hammond strongly favored Holiday, and Hammond had the final say. In addition to having Holiday at her best, in her prime, these remarkable Wilson records remain superb examples of Swing Era music. The musicians, including such great ones as Carter, Lester Young, Clayton, Eldridge, Hodges, and Chu Berry, were paid only union scale. Reissued and promoted as Billie Holiday recordings from her *Golden Years,* they are recommended especially to those who have the idea that Swing Era music was only big band music. The Wilson groups number seven or eight musicians, usually.

Although other jazz pianists, Wilson included, may have been more widely known, there is no question that the overwhelming favorite jazz pianist of jazz pianists was Art Tatum. He was also one of the few men of any trade, profession, or art who truly deserved the description "a legend in his own time."

Wilson was one of Tatum's greatest admirers. As he told me: "I liked Hines and Waller, but compared to Tatum, it seemed as though they were in a different field of activity." He continued:

Tatum was head and shoulders over all other jazz pianists and most classical pianists. He had the exceptional gift, the kind of ability that is very rare in people. He was almost like a man who could hit a home run every time at bat. He was a phenomenon. He brought an almost unbelievable degree of intense concentration to the piano, and he had a keyboard command that I have heard with no other jazz pianist and with very few classical pianists—possibly Walter Gieseking—and it went much further than that, much further than being a great technician. Art was uncanny.

There is little about Tatum's playing that hasn't been said before. Pianists in particular are quick to praise his touch, tone, speed, finger control, harmonic ingenuity, as well as his dazzling, breathtaking, nearly incredible runs all over the keyboard. He played tenths in his right hand as well as his left (left only is customary), and while running

Incredible—A word often used by other pianists to describe the piano playing of Art Tatum. (Photo by Bill Stern for Norman Granz's Clef Records.)

thirds in his right hand (instead of playing a single note) he played counter melodies with his left hand. Tatum often sounded as if he had four hands. Four *quick* hands. Some found his artistry too ornate, too overwhelming. But if he was too ornate, too overwhelming, perhaps he was too ornate, too overwhelming only in context, his context, like Shakespeare. In any event, Tatum was definitely not the kind of pianist some prominent jazz critics of a later generation would get excited about for playing "spare." Tatum was never spare.

A chat with Tatum in the early 1940s, at a small club in Washington called the Brown Derby, is memorable to me, but not because of what he said about music (including words of praise for Fats Waller). Because he could not sit at a table in the club (this was segregated Washington), after he finished a set he would move into a small closetlike booth created for black soloists. It was just big enough for the two of us and as he drank beer from a bottle he listened by portable radio to a ball game. He was not surprised nor concerned about the adulation he received, the loud applause as he was led to and from the bandstand and the rapt attention given as he played. His major interest that night was the ball game, which involved his team, the Detroit Tigers (Tatum was from Toledo, Ohio, near Detroit). He wanted my opinion as another baseball nut: could his Tigers win the pennant? His tremendous interest in baseball fascinated me because obviously—save for his mind's eye—Tatum had never truly seen a baseball game. He was completely blind in one eye and could just barely see a bit out of the other one.

Perhaps Art's blindness helped, not hindered, his piano playing. At least this was the opinion of Herman Chittison, a marvelous Swing Era pianist who was not as widely known as some because he was in Paris and Egypt from 1934–1942. Chittison knew Tatum from grammar school days in Toledo. One night in New York in 1967, Chittison told me: "I think Art's blindness had a great deal to do with his enormous skill. When the other kids in the neighborhood were out playing ball, Art was always at home practicing the piano."

John Eaton, the excellent Washington pianist, stressed to Tatum biographer James Lester that Tatum did not position his hands on the keyboard as most pianists do, that is with curved fingers and high wrists. Tatum's hands above the keyboard were almost horizontal from wrist to fingertips. Eaton suggested that the most accomplished pianists have discovered that flexibility, speed, and tone require flatter fingers and keeping the fingers closer to the keys. Vladimir Horowitz made that discovery and so did Art Tatum.

That may explain Tatum a bit, as does the practice, practice, and more practice idea suggested by Chittison. Still, there is probably no easy way to explain how a Tatum comes to be, save to say that he was, perhaps more than any other jazz musician, a musical genius. And who can explain genius?

Erroll Garner became much more famous during the 1950s but he arrived on Fifty-second Street from Pittsburgh at the tail end of the Swing Era during the 1940s. He was twenty-three years old when he first raised eyebrows on the Street, working with accomplished pros such as Slam Stewart. And the highly original, self-taught Garner always had the Swing Era in his heart and in his repertoire, certainly not more "modern" styles of jazz. He loved melody and was not about to be swept up by bop figurations and other new jazz fashions of the moment. He swung the bejesus out of a raft of old tunes others had forgotten or never knew, and for Erroll, as for most all of the great Swing Era players, jazz was most of all fun.

Unlike his two brothers and three sisters, he never learned to read music. Also, as I first discovered during conversation with him in 1966, Garner could not even read chord symbols (F9, for example). "I can find the chord you might want but I can't read it from a symbol or anything on paper," he said. Erroll also said he usually did not know what key he was in. This is why most of his bass players positioned themselves so that they could see Garner's hands on the keyboard, thus discovering the key. In his first professional dance band, Garner pretended to read music by looking at the music as he played. This ruse worked until a singer joined the band one night and brought along her own music for Erroll to play.

Years later, Ray Brown, a superb bass player, said: "Guys with Erroll Garner's talent don't have any fear of keys because they don't relate to keys, they relate to sounds. You don't know how difficult that is until you study music, and the more you study the more difficult F sharp gets." Garner sometimes played in such peculiar keys, for jazz, as E, A, or F sharp.

Until Garner, no one had ever played the piano the way he did. His playing was easily identified on a recording after only a few measures because of (1) his guitarlike left hand which was truly rhythmically exciting on an up-tempo tune, and (2) the delayed action or time lag in his right hand, playing melody, and sometimes in his left hand, too.

And how did Erroll develop that singular left hand? He told me: "Well, I listened to a guitar player friend of mine, that's one thing. But the real reason is because I couldn't read music. I had to find a way to accompany myself."

Garner had great rapport with his audience. "They feed me all the time," he said, talking about the way listeners could inspire him. This remark, typical of the man and his music, and indeed the Swing Era itself, pinpointed the vast difference between Garner and some of his bop era contemporaries (*not* Dizzy Gillespie) who acted as if an audience is a necessary evil, something a musician must somehow put up with to earn his daily bread.

The audience was important to Garner, as well as to his pocketbook, because communication was the name of his game. He played *for* people, not at them. Instead of looking at the keyboard as he played, he often watched the people watching him, enjoying the grins that resulted from his wily improvisations, impish expressions, and grunts.

His approach to the piano was orchestral, and he had a keen ear for dynamics. He also had a seemingly endless supply of seldom heard songs. As his drummer told me between sets one night: "I'm never surprised any more at what he might play. He knows all kinds of old tunes most of us have forgotten long ago and he's liable to go into any one of them just for kicks. I'm glad I'm his drummer and not his bass player."

Because he cherished Horowitz, Gieseking, and Tatum, and taught at Juilliard, one might think that Teddy Wilson would be slow to praise Garner. Not at all. Asked about Garner in 1958, Wilson replied: "Garner brought a great deal of originality to jazz piano, working with his time lag. His phrases come through with such conviction because they are his own. On the other hand, when you imitate another musician's way of playing and are too derivative, your phrases are not too clear, are just a shade vague, and they lack real conviction."

Decades after the Swing Era, when Garner romped into an old tune such as Ellington's almost forgotten *I've Got to Be a Rugcutter* ("and swing out, in the groove"), Erroll was helping to keep the spirit of the Swing Era alive. And also proving he was right when he told writer Ralph Gleason: "I know one thing I can really do, I can *swing!*"

Garner was one of the last of the Swing Era swingers.

When the Laughter Died

"For an era to end officially, you apparently need a corpus delecti. But it's when the laughter dies, not when a man's mortal remains become as one with the flowers of the field, that an era really ends." So wrote George Frazier in a 1973 newspaper column about Eddie Condon's death.

"When the laughter dies" is when an era really ends. That's an interesting thought and could be said of the Swing Era. When the laughter died, when jazz stopped being fun for many people, the Swing Era was over.

In reference to the French Revolution, Wordsworth wrote "Bliss was it in that dawn to be alive," adding "but to be young was very heaven!" Being young is of course not always "very heaven." But to be young during jazz music's golden age, the Swing Era, is remembered by some of us now in our seventies as a time of musical heaven, a time when jazz meant joy.

Sources

Jazz books feed off other jazz books, sometimes perpetuating myths by doing so, Stanley Dance has said, reasonably. The opinions in this book are my own, and many of the quotations by musicians were made to me, but this book has drawn upon other books and other printed matter, too. I trust no myths are repeated. Sources are listed by chapter. Magazine and newspaper essays by the author that include statements by musicians used in this book are presented in abbreviated or slightly different form.

1: When Jazz Was Popular, and Why

Asher, Don. *Notes From a Battered Grand* (New York: Harcourt Brace Jovanovich, 1992): 76.

Barnet, Charlie. *Those Swinging Years: The Autobiography of Charlie Barnet,* with Stanley Dance (Baton Rouge: Louisiana State University Press, 1984): 193.

Barron, Blue. "Swing Is Nothing But Sex," *Music & Rhythm* (August 1941). "Sweet Music Will Play at the Funeral of Swing!," *Music & Rhythm* (January 1942).

Dance, Stanley. *The World of Count Basie* (New York: Scribner's, 1980): 104 (Edison quote).

Down Beat. "Where the Bands Are Playing" (November and December issues, 1941). "BG Pays Pianist 2 Weeks Salary for 3 Numbers" (September 15, 1942).

Feather, Leonard. *The Encyclopedia of Jazz* (New York: Horizon Press, 1960).

Firestone, Ross. *Swing, Swing, Swing: The Life & Times of Benny Goodman* (New York: W. W. Norton, 1993).

Frazier, George. "Oh, What Has Befallen Boston of Fond Memory," *Boston Herald,* September 18, 1961, reprinted in part in *Another Man's Poison: The Life and Writing of George Frazier* by Charles Fountain (Chester, Conn.: Globe Pequot Press, 1984): 169.

Freeman, Bud. *Crazeology: The Autobiography of a Chicago Jazzman,* as told to Robert Wolf (Urbana: University of Illinois Press, 1989): 54.

Furia, Philip. *The Poets of Tin Pan Alley* (New York: Oxford University Press, 1990): 231 (Harry Warren quote).

Hammond, John. *John Hammond on Record,* with Irving Townsend (New York: Ridge Press/Summit Books, 1977): 168 (re Reno Club).

Krupa, Gene. The Krupa quotation, believed to have been originally in *Down Beat,* is from *Hear Me Talkin' to Ya,* ed. Nat Shapiro and Nat Hentoff (New York: Rinehart, 1955): 314–15.

Maxwell, Jimmy. On PBS-TV *American Masters* special "Benny Goodman: Adventures in the Kingdom of Swing."

McIntyre, Hal. Conversation with the author in Atlantic City, 1942.

Metronome, December 1941 issue.

_____. "Act of the Year, King Cole Trio" (January 1945): 15.

Morgenstern, Dan. *Jazz People* (New York: Harry N. Abrams, 1976): 145 (re golden age of jazz).

Music & Rhythm. "Why Bandsmen Crash and Die on One-Nighters" (August 1941).

Powell, Mel. LP liner notes, *Benny Goodman, Vol. 2, Live at Basin Street,* Musicmasters, Yale Music Library, 1988.

Scanlan, Tom. "'Trouble Is We've Lost the Kids,' Says Woody," *Army Times* (December 13, 1958).

_____. "The Impeccable Mr. Wilson" (*Down Beat,* January 22, 1959).

_____. "Benny Goodman, the Swing Era, and Me," 30th anniversary issue of *Down Beat* (July 2, 1964).

_____. "Three Men on Six Strings" (*Down Beat,* August 1, 1963), (Byrd quote).

Shaw, Arnold. *The Street That Never Slept: New York's Fabled 52d St.* (New York: Coward, McCann & Geoghegan, 1971), especially chapter 20, "Death of a Street."

Simon, George T. *The Big Bands* (New York: Macmillan, 1967): including Will Bradley quote, 97.

Wilder, Alec. *American Popular Song: The Great Innovaters, 1900–1950,* with James T. Maher (New York: Oxford University Press, 1972).

2: *White, Black, Brown, and Beige*

Barnet. Op. cit.: 93, 95, 122.

Basie, Count. *Good Morning Blues: The Autobiography of Count Basie,* as told to Albert Murray (New York: Random House, 1985).

Bigard, Barney. *With Louis and the Duke,* ed. Barry Martyn. (New York: Oxford University Press, 1986): a, 11, 32, 38 (1988 edition).

Calloway, Cab, and Bryant Rollins. *Of Minnie the Moocher and Me* (New York: Thomas Y. Crowell, 1976): 41–42, 88, 129, 146, 155 (Payne quote).

Demaris, Ovid. "I Learned About Forgiveness," *Parade* (November 7, 1993), (interview with Natalie Cole).

Firestone. Op. cit.: 164, 166, 312.

Fox, Ted. *Showtime at the Apollo* (New York: Da Capo Press, 1993).

Freeman. Op. cit.: 7, 13–14.

_____. *You Don't Look Like a Musician* (Detroit: Belamp, 1974): 102–03.

Hammond. Op. cit.: 194 (re Earle Warren).

Hinton, Milt, and David G. Berger. *Bass Line: The Stories and Photographs of Milt Hinton* (Philadelphia: Temple University Press, 1988): 15.

Horne, Lena, and Richard Schickle. *Lena* (New York: Signet, 1966): 45, 99, 109. (hardcover: Doubleday, 1965).

Kirk, Andy. *Twenty Years on Wheels* as told to Amy Lee (Ann Arbor: University of Michigan Press, 1989): 114.

Scanlan, Tom. "Meet a Superb Trumpet Player," *Army Times* (June 21, 1962), (re Fulcher).

_____. "The Impeccable Mr. Wilson," op. cit.

Singer, Barry. *Black and Blue: The Life and Lyrics of Andy Razaf* (New York: Schirmer Books, 1992).

Wilson, Douglas L. "Thomas Jefferson and the Character Issue," *Atlantic* (November 1962).

Wilson, John S. "Meet Professor Carter," *Down Beat* (April 2, 1969).

3: Dozens of Great Players

Barnet. Op. cit.: 14 (Armstrong), 80 (Hodges).

Dance, Stanley. Booklet with *The Complete Lionel Hampton, 1937–1941,* Bluebird boxed LP set AXM6-5536.

Doran, James M. *Erroll Garner: The Most Happy Piano* (Metuchen, N.J.: Scarecrow Press and Institute of Jazz Studies, Rutgers University, 1985): 38 (Brown quote).

Estice, Wayne, and Paul Rubin. *Jazz Spoken Here: Conversations With Twenty-Two Musicians* (Baton Rouge: Louisiana State University Press, 1992): 94 (Bryant quote).

Feather, Leonard. *The Book of Jazz: A Guide to the Entire Field* (New York: Horizon Press, 1957): especially 61 (re Hines).

Frazier, George. "The Friends of Eddie Condon," *Boston Globe* (August 13, 1979).

Gleason, Ralph J. "Erroll Garner" in *Jam Session: An Anthology of Jazz,* ed. Gleason (New York: G. P. Putnam's Sons, 1958): 170.

Hammond. Op. cit.: 223–24 (re Christian).

Hampton, Lionel, as told to Bernard Seeman. "Me and Benny Goodman," *Saturday Evening Post* (December 18, 1954).

Hentoff, Nat. "The Man Who Used Jazz for Justice," *The Washington Post* (May 7, 1994), (Granz on Eldridge).

Jordan, Steve, with Tom Scanlan. *Rhythm Man: Fifty Years in Jazz* (Ann Arbor: University of Michigan Press, 1991): 148.

Lester, James. *Too Marvelous for Words: The Life and Genius of Art Tatum* (New York: Oxford University Press, 1994): 7 (Wilson), 88 (Eaton).

Morgenstern. Op. cit.: 133 (re Davison).

Pepper, Art and Laurie. *Straight Life: The Story of Art Pepper* (New York: Schimer Books, 1979).

Scanlan, Tom. Jazz Music columns in *Army Times:* On death of Tatum, November 17, 1956. "Benny Carter Is One of the Few 'Greats,' " February 7, 1959. "Django Was Fantastic," September 1, 1965. "Thanks, Fats," November 3, 1965. "About the President" (on Lester Young), January 12, 1966. "Between Sets With Roy," February 9, 1966. "Between Sets With Pee Wee," June 6, 1966. "Erroll Garner Plays Joy," August 31, 1966. "Blues for Ed Hall and Muggsy," March 1, 1967. "He Had Rhythm, Melody, Cigars" (on Chittison), March 19, 1967. "There'll Never Be Another Stuff," November 1, 1967. "A Few Words, Now, on Music" (on Wilson), January 3, 1968. "Fats Is Still With Us," January 24, 1968. "Only One Pee Wee," March 5, 1969. "The Hawk's Upstairs," June 4, 1969. "He Made a Man Out of Jazz" (on Armstrong), July 28, 1971. "Blues for Charlie Shavers," August 4, 1971. "Louis Said: 'Bunny' " (on Berigan), May 3, 1972.

_____. "Jazz Journal" (on jazz drummers), *American Weekend* (November 17, 1956).

_____. "The Impeccable Mr. Wilson," op cit.

_____. "About the Death of an Artist" (on Ben Webster), *Federal Times* (October 10, 1973).

_____. "About Bobby" (on Hackett), Editor's Corner, *Federal Times* (June 21, 1976).

Wilber, Bob, assisted by Derek Webster, *Music Was Not Enough* (New York: Oxford University Press, 1987): 81–82 (on Goodman).

Additional Reading

There are currently hundreds of books that involve, directly or indirectly, the Swing Era. Those listed below are only some of the most interesting. Many of these have been reprinted in paperback, often by a different publisher, but this list usually refers only to the original books. And even most of those that have been out-of-print for years can be found in good libraries. Comments in this critical bibliography do not always represent majority views.

Allen, Walter C. *Hendersonia: The Music of Fletcher Henderson and His Musicians*. Highland Park, N.J.: 1973. Later reprinted by Institute of Jazz Studies.

Henderson (1897–1952) led the first big band that really mattered, and his later work for Goodman helped to bring about the Swing Era. A hefty book (651 pages) that is mainly facts. One of the great jazz discographies.

Balliett, Whitney. *56 Portraits in Jazz*. New York: Oxford University Press, 1986.

A prose stylist with keen eyes and ears for meaningful detail, Balliett also knows how to edit lengthy interviews for maximum effect. This book contains all of his *New Yorker* biographical pieces on jazz musicians written from 1962 to early 1986. Many are Swing Era stars, including Hackett (who "talks in a deep, soft monotone fretted by a Providence drawl, which falls somewhere between a Brooklyn accent and a South Boston one"), Cheatham, Stacy, Eldridge, and Bushkin. (Other similar, smaller collections of Balliett jazz pieces are also recommended, but the reader is advised to wonder about some of Balliett's sweeping opinions and air of certitude that can rankle when, for example, he ranks musicians as first- or second-rate.)

Barnet, Charlie, with Stanley Dance. *Those Swinging Years: The Autobiography of Charlie Barnet.* **Baton Rouge: Louisiana State University Press, 1984.**

Rings true throughout and inspires laughter frequently. Subject matter is not wine, women, and song, but Scotch, women, and jazz. Although Barnet was married a dozen or more times (most were simply "alcoholic mistakes," says Charlie) and a close friend of numerous ladies of the evening, this book—in delightful contrast to other show biz memoirs that report sexual escapading—has no sex scenes, no dirty words, no kiss and tell, no attempt to be titillating. Many provocative comments on music plus funny stories make this one of the best of all jazz autobiographies.

Basie, Count, as told to Albert Murray. *Good Morning Blues: The Autobiography of Count Basie.* **New York: Random House, 1985.**

Basie died before this was published. Contains unnecessary padding but there is much of great interest involving Basie's Swing Era band.

Berger, Morroe, with Edward Berger and James Patrick. *Benny Carter: A Life in American Music.* **2 vols. Metuchen, N.J.: Scarecrow Press and Institute of Jazz Studies, Rutgers University, 1982.**

Much research by the late Princeton sociology professor but it is the comments by Carter that make the book valuable. There is far too much questionable pedantic material that does not pertain to Carter in the first volume's second half. Second volume is mainly an exceptional discography compiled by Edward Berger, Morroe's oldest son, and also includes an index of Carter's compositions and arrangements by year (from 1927 to publication date) and a seventy-six-page summary of his recorded work as arranger and composer. (At this writing, the amazing Carter, born in 1907, is still playing.)

Calloway, Cab, and Bryant Rollins. *Of Minnie the Moocher and Me.* **New York: Thomas Y. Crowell, 1976.**

Cotton Club days, the road, racial problems, and his excellent band of the early 1940s.

Chilton, John. *Sidney Bechet: The Wizard of Jazz.* **New York: Oxford University Press, 1987.**

Like other Chilton books, there is no psychobabble, just the facts, with much about Bechet's recordings.

_____. *The Song of the Hawk: The Life and Recordings of Coleman Hawkins.* Ann Arbor: University of Michigan Press, 1990.

Good if unexciting biography of the great tenor saxophone player. A few of the comments by Hawkins may surprise some.

_____. *Who's Who of Jazz: Storyville to Swing Street.* New York: Da Capo Press, 1985. Several earlier editions, beginning in 1972.

All musicians and "vocalists" given individual entries were born before 1920. More than 1,000 musicians, some not included in Leonard Feather's better-known *Encyclopedia of Jazz.* Emphasis is on facts, not opinion. Useful for discovering what musicians played with whom when.

Clayton, Buck, assisted by Nancy Miller Elliott. *Buck Clayton's Jazz World.* New York: Oxford University Press, 1987. Originally published by Macmillan Press Ltd., London, 1986.

Not as well edited as it should have been, but contains many marvelous passages, provocative views of other musicians, and just misses being one of the best jazz autobiographies. (It took Buck a long, long time to find a willing publisher, which he finally found in England. He told me that at one time he "considered throwing the entire thing into the Atlantic Ocean.")

Collier, James Lincoln. *Duke Ellington.* New York: Oxford University Press, 1987.

As demonstrated in his earlier books, *The Making of Jazz* and *Louis Armstrong: An American Genius* (but not in his so-so Goodman biography), Collier has been bitten by the psychobiography bug. And in this book Collier also indulges in his habit of persistent, sometimes ludicrous, speculation. Still, despite such obvious faults, the jazz writer Ellingtonians love to hate presents some reasonable and refreshing criticism of now-icon Duke. He contends Ellington took credit for the musical work of others (he would of course not be the first bandleader to do so) and wrote some terribly dull and pretentious music as his fame increased. Collier is also surprised that Ellington "never made an effort to study the whole tradition of Western music." So maybe Ellington was simply too busy with his own distinctive music and his own unquestionably great orchestra.

Condon, Eddie, with narration by Thomas Sugrue. *We Called It Music: A Generation of Jazz.* **New York: Henry Holt, 1947.**

Includes some funny and meaningful Condon stories.

Connor, D. Russell. *Benny Goodman: Listen to His Legacy.* **Metuchen, N.J.: Scarecrow Press and Institute of Jazz Studies, 1988.**

This large book, with essential facts about thousands of Goodman recordings, is one of the great jazz discographies. The records date from his first recording session with Ben Pollack's band in 1926 at age sixteen. He had been a professional musician for three years at that time. (There were two earlier versions of this amazing discography: *BG On the Record*, with Warren W. Hicks, New Rochelle: Arlington House, 1969, and the original, self-published *BG Off the Record* by Connor, Fairless Hills, Pa.: Gaildonna, 1958.)

Dance, Stanley. *The World of Count Basie.* **New York: Scribner's, 1980.**

Interviews with Basie musicians including some from Swing Era days. Many quotable, meaningful words by Jo Jones, Harry Edison, Dicky Wells, Buck Clayton, Earle Warren, Jimmy Rushing, others.

_____. *The World of Duke Ellington.* **New York: Scribner's, 1970.**

Not a biography, but certainly one of the best books on Ellington, his music, his musicians. Mainly interviews with Ellington players, and a few with Ellington, too.

_____. *The World of Earl Hines.* **New York: Scribner's, 1977.**

More interesting interviews, with Hines and Budd Johnson included.

_____. *The World of Swing.* **New York: Scribner's, 1974.**

Another fine collection of previously published taped interviews judiciously edited. The several dozen Swing Era musicians involved include such major players as Hawkins, Carter, Goodman, Hampton, Eldridge, and many lesser-known players (e.g., Ed Wilcox, Jimmy Crawford, arranger Andy Gibson). Recommended but—for whatever reason—this world of swing is woefully incomplete because no white Swing Era musician, aside from Goodman, is among those interviewed.

Deffaa, Chip. *Swing Legacy.* **Metuchen, N.J.: Scarecrow Press and Institute of Jazz Studies, 1989.**

Though born in 1951, Deffaa has great affection for Swing Era music. Interviews, most previously published, with Stéphane Grappelli, Johnny Blowers, Artie Shaw, Chris Griffin, Lee Castle (Castaldo), Panama Francis, Woody Herman.

Feather, Leonard. *The Book of Jazz: A Guide to the Entire Field.* **New York: Horizon Press, 1957.**

Still one of the best introductions to jazz. The dozen chapters on the major players of the various instruments are extremely well done. Mostly facts, but some opinion, too.

_____. *The Encyclopedia of Jazz.* **New York: Horizon Press, 1960.**

There have been later, smaller "yearbook" additions to this enormously useful encyclopedia (first edition in 1955), but for Swing Era players the 1960 volume (more than 500 pages) is the one to find. Although this is a monumental work deserving great praise, it is easy to grumble about who was left out and who was put in (Elvis Presley, of all people, is included!). And there is considerable opinion expressed by Feather or his editorial helpers amidst the biographical facts. For example, in the Gillespie entry, it is stated that bop was "a melodic, harmonic, and rhythmic advancement of jazz," a view that can certainly be questioned, with emphasis on the words *melodic, rhythmic,* and *advancement.* Still, this is surely the most valuable reference book on jazz musicians ever published. All jazz enthusiasts need this one.

Ferguson, Otis. *The Otis Ferguson Reader.* **Edited by Dorothy Chamberlain and Robert Wilson. Highland Park, Ill.: December Press, 1982.**

Ferguson, a book reviewer and movie critic for *The New Republic* from 1933 until 1942, also wrote some superb essays on jazz and most everything he wrote on the music is here. Included are pieces on the Savoy Ballroom, Goodman, Stacy, Elman, Ellington, and an uncommon, thoughtful, highly critical view of John Hammond. Jazz lost one of its finest critics in 1943 when Ferguson, at age 34, was killed during World War II.

Firestone, Ross. *Swing, Swing, Swing: The Life & Times of Benny Goodman*. New York: W. W. Norton, 1993.

Easily the best book on Goodman, and one of the finest of all jazz biographies. Carefully written, well researched, and enlivened by interviews with former BG musicians and others who knew him.

Fountain, Charles. *Another Man's Poison: The Life and Writing of Columnist George Frazier*. Chester, Conn.: Globe Pequot Press, 1984.

Includes good examples of Frazier's jazz writing, which had style, grace, strong opinion. His writing was certainly not limited to jazz, but his heart, often apparent in his work, was always with the music.

Fox, Ted. *Showtime at the Apollo*. New York: Holt, Rinehart, and Winston, 1983.

This history of Harlem's famous theater on 125th Street has much about the music scene during the 1930s and 1940s. In addition to singers, comics, and tap dancers, dozens of swing bands played the Apollo. One night as Lionel Hampton's band swung *Flying Home,* a young man stood on a balcony rail shouting "I'm flying, I'm flying," then tested his wings into the orchestra section below. No one was hurt, but this incident is the reason Jerry Valentine entitled a piece for the Earl Hines band *Second Balcony Jump*.

Freeman, Bud, as told to Robert Wolf. *Crazeology: The Autobiography of a Chicago Jazzman*. Urbana: University of Illinois Press, 1989.

_____. *You Don't Look Like a Musician*. Detroit: Belamp, 1974.

These two small books by tenor saxophonist Freeman (1906–1991) combine to be one of the best of all jazz memoirs. They add up to little more than 200 pages but there is something of interest or delight on nearly every page. Information about jazz in Chicago during the 1920s, jazz in New York during the 1930s and 1940s, plus provocative, witty opinions on the music, and some unquestionably funny stories.

Giddens, Gary. *Riding on a Blue Note: Jazz & American Pop*. New York: Oxford University Press, 1981.

The able jazz critic of *The Village Voice* is too young to recall the Swing Era, but several of his interesting essays here relate to it in some way, including pieces on Teagarden, Venuti, Basie, and pianist David Lambert. "Goodman once told me he was shocked to see the target audience of pop performers decreasing in age, decade by decade, so that in the '70s the mass taste is defined by fourteen-year-olds," Giddens reports. And in reference to Gillespie's pre-bop days, Dizzy tells him this about Eldridge: "We tried to play just like him, but I never did quite make it."

Gottlieb, William P. *The Golden Age of Jazz*. New York: Simon & Schuster, 1979.

Many good photos of Swing Era musicians, taken between 1939 and 1948, most for *Down Beat*.

Hajdu, David. *Lush Life: A Biography of Billy Strayhorn*. New York: Farrar, Straus, Giroux, 1996.

Superb biography of the great composer Strayhorn (1915–1967), whose sterling work was so important to the Ellington band. Hajdu says he spent "more than three thousand hours of conversation over the course of eleven years" doing research for this book and that's easy to believe. In the small world of jazz scholarship, this book was badly needed. Highly recommended.

Hammond, John, with Irving Townsend. *John Hammond on Record*. New York: Ridge Press/Summit Books, 1977.

Autobiography of the son of a Vanderbilt who became a relentless fighter for racial equality when it was not fashionable and also an enthusiastic promoter of jazz as critic, record producer, and unpaid talent scout during the Swing Era. Many opinions on the great and near-great, whom he knew and recorded, including Goodman (who became his brother-in-law in 1942), Basie, Young, Holiday, Clayton, Christian, Mildred Bailey.

Hasse, John Edward. *Beyond Category: The Life and Genius of Duke Ellington*. New York: Simon & Schuster, 1993.

Unmistakable cheerleading view, as the title suggests. Hasse gathers together much information on the Duke and his players from many printed sources and presents it all well.

Hinton, Milt, and David G. Berger. *Bass Line: The Stories and Photographs of Milt Hinton*. Philadelphia: Temple University Press, 1988.

Extraordinary book of bright prose and fine photos of jazz musicians by the great bass player who has worked with just about everybody. Photos date from his days on the road with the Calloway band. And the Judge's commentary is perceptive and informative. (At this writing, Hinton, born in 1910, is still playing, still showing many a younger man how.)

Jordan, Steve, with Tom Scanlan. *Rhythm Man: Fifty Years in Jazz.* **Ann Arbor: University of Michigan Press, 1991.**

Funny stories, and a few poignant ones, about the famous and not-so-famous musicians this excellent big and small band rhythm guitarist worked with from 1939 on.

Kirk, Andy, as told to Amy Lee. *Twenty Years on Wheels.* **Ann Arbor: University of Michigan Press, 1989.**

Pleasant, appealing, modest report of what it was like leading one of the Swing Era's better black bands. To avoid booking confusion, his band was to be called "Andy Kirk and His Dark Clouds of Joy," but Kirk wouldn't stand for that and dropped the "Dark," thus his "Twelve Clouds of Joy." These Clouds played in 300 cities, with $3,000 the highest pay for a one-nighter (a "June German" festival in Rocky Mount, North Carolina). Not much here about his most famous "Cloud of Joy," pianist and arranger Mary Lou Williams.

Lees, Gene. *Leader of the Band: The Life of Woody Herman.* **New York: Oxford University Press, 1995.**

Informative, sympathetic biography of the popular bandleader. Includes fascinating quotes from Herman's musical colleagues Ralph Burns, Neal Hefti, Terry Gibbs, Phil Wilson, Bill Chase, Milt Jackson, Lou Levy, many others. Much about Woody's sad and infuriating problems with the IRS, brought on by a manager who liked to gamble. And anyone who may have wondered about that title, *Lady McGowan's Dream,* must read this book. Recommended although Lees is quick to use the perpendicular pronoun which often puts the reader's focus on Lees, not his subject matter.

Lester, James. *Too Marvelous for Words: The Life and Genius of Art Tatum.* **New York: Oxford University Press, 1994.**

Informative and long-overdue biography of the most amazing of all jazz pianists.

McCarthy, Albert. *Big Band Jazz.* **New York: Berkley Windhover, 1977. Originally published by Carter Nash Cameron, England, 1974.**

A major achievement and required reading for big band enthusiasts. Lots of photos. Much attention given, refreshingly, to less famous bands. Mostly facts, but there is opinion (e.g., "it seems apparent that Charlie Barnet's Bluebird output of 1939–1942 represents the most consistently excellent jazz music produced by any white swing band of its period," an obvious dismissal of the Goodman band and a view not "apparent" to many who heard Swing Era music in America.

Morgan, Norman. *The History of the Guitar in Jazz*. New York: Oak Publications, 1983.

Includes music and more than 200 photos. Swing Era players not forgotten, including some rhythm men such as Reuss, Green, Jordan. (And Christian could not have read the transcribed notes of his improvised solo on manuscript here simply because Charlie could not read music.)

Morgenstern, Dan, with photographs by Ole Brask. *Jazz People*. New York: Harry N. Abrams, 1976.

Large, handsomely produced coffee-table book with great photos by Brask and knowledgeable prose by Morgenstern. Much about Swing Era musicians. Highly recommended.

Porter, Lewis, ed. *A Lester Young Reader*. Washington, D.C.: Smithsonian Institution Press, 1991.

Assorted essays on Young. Among the best are those by John Hammond, Loren Schoenberg, Nat Hentoff, and Leonard Feather.

Schuller, Gunther. *The Swing Era: The Development of Jazz, 1930–1945*. New York: Oxford University Press, 1989.

Listed because many seem to have a high regard for Schuller's jazz criticism and because this is probably the largest single volume on the Swing Era (more than 900 pages). It is not, however, a history, musical or otherwise, of the period. It is one man's opinion of many Swing Era recordings, interspersed with comments on the musicians involved. These comments range from astute to absurd. While writing this book, called "monumental" by some reviewers, Schuller says he listened to "some 30,000 recordings" and perhaps that alone earns him attention as well as commiseration.

Not a jazz player but a French horn player and classical music conductor and composer (he won the Pulitzer Prize for formal musical composition in 1994) and teacher too, Schuller shows his formal music bias throughout this book, with composition usually placed on a much higher plateau than improvisation.

There are many Schuller views to cheer, but some will find Schuller opinions to question on nearly every other page. He baffles with such statements as: "one must realize that dynamics have always played a minor role in jazz," Goodman "is not profound in the way we feel Beethoven and Charlie Parker are profound," and "jazz in its modern garb moved way past [Art Tatum], whose influence in creative terms … was modest."

Schuller is much more at home with "modern" players (and he assumes an evolutionary view of jazz, thus later is necessarily greater), explaining and defending his "third stream" music or extolling the marvels and profundities to be discovered in the music of Parker, Mingus, Coltrane, and Ornette Coleman.

In the appendix, Schuller presents what he calls a scientific demonstration of what swings and what doesn't, with sounds analyzed by computer. This is unconvincing, totally bewildering. The book does include more than 500 musical examples and there are keen judgments to be found here and there amidst all the strange pronouncements from on high.

Shapiro, Nat, and Nat Hentoff, eds. *The Jazz Makers.* **New York: Rinehart, 1957.**

Twenty-one essays on different players, most Swing Era musicians. Among the best: Hentoff on Young and Eldridge, Charles Edward Smith on Teagarden and Russell, John S. Wilson on Hines, and Leonard Feather on Hawkins.

Shaw, Arnold. *The Street That Never Slept: New York's Fabled 52d St.* **New York: Coward, McCann & Geoghegan, 1971.**

Excellent book on the clubs where so much great jazz was played during the Swing Era. Fascinating detail on the Onyx, the Famous Door, Kelly's Stables, the Three Deuces, Jimmy Ryan's, Hickory House, and other jazz joints on what musicians and jazz fans called "The Street."

Simon, George T. *The Big Bands.* **New York: Macmillan, 1967.**

Good book about the big bands of the Swing Era, including the corny orchestras, too. The veteran *Metronome* writer and editor (younger brother of Richard Simon, cofounder of Simon & Schuster) made great use of his old reviews. Also many photos from that magazine. Hundreds of big bands are included, dating from 1935 through 1946.

_____. *Glenn Miller and His Orchestra*. New York: Thomas Y. Crowell, 1974.

For those who enjoyed Miller's music, written by a fan and friend of the bandleader.

Smith, Willie "The Lion," with George Hoefer. *Music on My Mind: The Memoirs of an American Pianist*. Garden City, N.Y.: Doubleday, 1964.

Among the best of all jazz memoirs. Smith was a fascinating pianist and a remarkable man who had a lot to say and who said it in an original way. Also remarkable is the fact that Hoefer did not take notes nor use a tape recorder to produce this minor masterpiece. As he told me: "He'd talk. I'd listen. Then I'd go home and write down what he had said. I began to think and talk like him!" The Lion's "vibrations" and the positions of the planets must have been right when he and Hoefer decided to do this book.

Stearns, Marshall, and Jean Stearns. *Jazz Dance and the Story of American Vernacular Dance*. New York: Macmillan, 1968.

Excellent book on "American dancing that is performed to and with the rhythms of jazz—that is, dancing that swings." Read all about the shim sham, the lindy hop, the shorty George, etc. Infinitely superior to Marshall Stearns's widely read *The Story of Jazz*, a strange jazz history book that kisses off the Swing Era in twenty pages.

Stewart, Rex. *Boy Meets Horn*. Edited by Claire P. Gordon. Ann Arbor: University of Michigan Press, 1991.

Excellent autobiography. Stewart's early days in Washington, then with Henderson, McKinney's Cotton Pickers, and Ellington. Sample quote: "I view with deep concern and genuine alarm the catastrophic decline of jazz music in the country of its origin." The famous cornetist says jazz is about "melody and beat" and is supposed to bring "happiness and joy" with "sounds pleasant to the human ear." Amen, Rex.

_____. *Jazz Masters of the Thirties*. New York: Macmillan, 1972.

Collection of twenty previously published magazine pieces. Perceptive, well-written comments on some great jazz players, including Armstrong, Henderson, Harrison, Hawkins, Norvo, Ellington, Carter, Catlett, Tatum. A superb book, published after Stewart's death in 1967.

Stokes, W. Royal, with photo preparation by Don Peterson. *Swing Era New York: The Jazz Photographs of Charles Peterson.* **Philadelphia: Temple University Press, 1994.**

More than 200 candid shots by Charles Peterson, who left professional guitar playing to become one of the finest photographers of Swing Era musicians. His son Don carefully restored the photos from negatives, and Stokes did much painstaking research to identify the lesser-known players.

Tucker, Mark. *The Duke Ellington Reader.* **New York: Oxford University Press, 1993.**

Good collection of essays on Ellington. (Another Tucker book, *Ellington: The Early Years,* Urbana, Ill.: University of Illinois Press, 1991, is scholarly, never dull, and musically aware, but is not listed in this bibliography because it does not involve the Swing Era. The book ends with the Ellington band's debut at the Cotton Club on December 4, 1927.)

Wells, Dicky, as told to Stanley Dance. *The Night People.* **Boston: Crescendo, 1971.**

Inside info from Basie's Swing Era trombonist, ranging from the music of Basie, et al., to related matter (e.g., "Earl [Hines] told one of his guys once, 'You may have holes in your shoes, but don't let the people out front know it. Shine the tops.' "

Wilder, Alec. *American Popular Song: The Great Innovators, 1900–1950.* **Edited by James T. Maher. New York: Oxford University Press, 1972.**

A most valuable study of American popular music (before rock), the blood and bone of so much glorious jazz. This book is provocative, informative, opinionated, never dull. Maher's fine writing hand is apparent throughout. Composer Wilder discusses the work of nearly 200 song writers, zeroing in on more than 3,500 measures of music from more than 700 songs. And yes, some great songs are not included (e.g., Eubie Blake's *Memories of You*). About half the book is devoted to the work of six composers: Kern, Berlin (who would not permit a single measure from any of his songs to be reproduced in this book), Gershwin, Rodgers, Porter, and Arlen. This volume will, properly, remain in print for a long time. Highly recommended.

Recommended Recordings

This list includes some of the best Swing Era jazz music recordings on LP, cassette, and compact disc. Most of it comes from 78rpm records. There are also some broadcast "airchecks."

Enormous improvement in recording has been made since the 1940s, and some music listed here, marvelous though it may be, is not presented with high fidelity. Several Art Tatum recordings, for example, symbolize low fidelity as well as lofty artistry. Of course music lovers believe, rightly, that great music poorly reproduced is highly preferable to mediocre music presented by the finest sound reproduction.

Recorded sound varies on reissues, including those on compact disc (CD), for many reasons, one major reason being the ears and musical tastes of those controlling the reproduction process. As is painfully apparent on too many big band reissues, highs (trumpets) and lows (bass) are unduly emphasized, diminishing or simply overwhelming the all-important middle sounds (reeds). And some have noticed that the sound on some cassettes is clearly inferior to the sound on the original shellac 78s, on vinyl LPs, or on open reel tapes. Also, as some so-called "vinylheads" will be quick to tell you, compact disc sound is not always better than LP sound. Digital remastering is often superb, a major step forward, but one need not be a recording engineer to know that remastering, digitally or not, is tricky and challenging. Not everyone who does it is good at it. Some older reissues were produced, necessarily and unnecessarily, by simply rerecording old records, occasionally complete with surface noise.

Although all recordings listed were made during the 1930s and 1940s, with a few as late as 1948 (e.g., by Woody Herman's "Second Herd"), anyone interested in the jazz music of the Swing Era is reminded that many superb recordings by Swing Era players were made after 1948. Dozens of LPs could be cited to prove this point. A few examples:

One of Jack Teagarden's best recorded sets, *Jazz Ultimate* (Capitol 933), with Bobby Hackett, was produced in 1957. *Swinging the Thirties* (Contemporary 334), a 1958 LP, is a splendid example of the exceptional Benny Carter and the exceptional Earl Hines. *Mel Powell Septet* (Vanguard 8004), superbly recorded in 1953, has compelling solos by Powell, Buck Clayton, and Ed Hall plus the kind of cohesive rhythm section seldom heard today. And a marvelous, crackling example of great trumpet playing by Roy Eldridge can be found on Illinois Jacquet's *Swing's the Thing* (Verve 8023), one of many excellent LPs featuring Swing Era players produced by Norman Granz during post–Swing Era years when bop, not swing, entranced most jazz record producers. Indeed, the best recordings by some Swing Era players—Ben Webster, Red Norvo, Sweets Edison, and many others including nonpareil singer Ella Fitzgerald—were made after 1948.

Not all of the recordings listed below are easy to find. This is especially true of the LPs. Record companies have an understandable habit of deleting reissue albums that do not sell, and many companies—including jazz labels—have stopped LP production entirely. Many large record stores no longer even carry LPs. Meanwhile, a jazz reissue label, Mosaic, is not only producing vinyl but is bringing back deep groove heavy vinyl discs because those capture the warm vibrant sound of the original 78s better than thinner LPs or even CDs.

Serious collectors of Swing Era music may still need to visit second-hand record stores or contact jazz LP dealers by mail, but more and more Swing Era music is becoming available on CD every year. This good news means that this list will soon be somewhat out-of-date. Who knows what fine Swing Era music, now only in 78rpm grooves, might suddenly become available on CD? Or, thanks to Mosaic and others, even on LP? As for the major record companies, holding the rights to so much good swing music, what will be reissued remains, as ever, not only a matter of taste and musical quality but a matter of fashion and sales potential.

There is considerable duplication of old records on different cassettes and CDs, and LP reissue titles are sometimes changed on CD versions of the same 78rpm records. CD and cassette reproduction of 78s, a welcome happening for jazz lovers, is not soon to end but no doubt will remain a quirky, ploddingly slow process.

Some recordings listed below only as LPs may now also be available on cassette (C) or compact disc (CD). Before searching for any LP listed below, the reader who favors cassette or CD recordings, as most readers probably do, is urged to check with cassette and CD experts, meaning those armed with informative computers, to discover if the music desired may be on tape or CD.

For more comprehensive lists of Swing Era recordings, there are many overall jazz discographies to study. These include more than five thousand pages of Tom Lord's ongoing monumental compilation *The Jazz Discography*. At this writing, Lord is not a third of the way through the alphabet but has produced nine volumes, each numbering around 600 pages (Cadence Jazz Books: Redwood, N.Y.). A total of twenty-five volumes is planned to reach Bob Zurke and anyone else alphabetically behind him. There are also good discographies of prominent individual musicians (Ellington is a favorite subject, especially in Europe). And two recent softcover, easy-to-find reference books include much information on many Swing Era recordings that are more or less available: *The Penguin Guide to Jazz on CD, LP & Cassette,* by Richard Cook and Brian Norton (London: Penguin Books, 1992), and *All Music Guide to Jazz: The Best CDs, Albums & Tapes,* edited by Ron Wynn, (San Francisco: Miller Freeman Books, 1994).

One more note: Swing Era record sales and popularity polls or "current majority critical opinion," whatever that may be, had absolutely nothing to do with the list below.

Small Groups and Piano Solos

LOUIS ARMSTRONG
- *Pops: 1940's Small Band Sides* (Bluebird 6378). CD.
- *Satchmo at Symphony Hall, Vols. 1–2* (Decca 195 and 8038). Two LPs.
  Many of Armstrong's greatest records were made before, and some after, the Swing Era.

SIDNEY BECHET
- *Sidney Bechet, 1932–43: The Bluebird Sessions* (Bluebird 90317). Five CDs.
- *The Complete Blue Note Recordings of Sidney Bechet* (Mosaic 110). Six LPs, five CDs.
  This heartfelt swinger could not read music but as the ghosts of Johnny Hodges, Duke Ellington, and others would be quick to agree, it didn't matter.

CHU BERRY
- *Giants of the Tenor Sax* (Commodore 7004). LP, C, CD. (Also includes a Lucky Thompson group.)
- *Indispensable* (Bluebird 89481). LP.
  Roy Eldridge is his swinging colleague on the first one listed. Chu (formally, Leon), a great player, is too often forgotten or ignored in many

jazz history books. He is also on some of the Wilson-Holiday and Hampton recordings listed below.

ROY ELDRIDGE

- *On Keynote* (PolyGram 830923). LP.
  With Coleman Hawkins on some tracks. Eldridge is also on other recommended recordings listed including some of the Wilson-Holiday gems. For his big band work, check out *Little Jazz* (CBS 465684, CD), *After You've Gone* (Decca 16052, CD) or *Uptown* (Columbia 45448, CD), with Gene Krupa's band and singer Anita O'Day.

DUKE ELLINGTON

- *Duke's Men: Small Groups—Vols. 1–2* (Columbia 46995, 48835). Each volume has two CDs.
- *The Great Ellington Units* (Bluebird 6751). CD.
  Marvelous music by Rex Stewart, Johnny Hodges, Barney Bigard, Cootie Williams, Lawrence Brown, and other Ellington players.

BUD FREEMAN

- *Jammin' at Commodore* (Commodore 7007). LP, C, CD.
  With Eddie Condon and friends including Pee Wee Russell, Jess Stacy, Bobby Hackett.

BENNY GOODMAN

- *Original Trio and Quartet Sessions, Vols. 1–2* (Bluebird 5631, 2273). CDs.
- *Goodman Sextet Featuring Charlie Christian* (Columbia 45144). CD.
- *Small Groups 1941–1945* (Columbia 44437). CD.
- *Slipped Disc 1945–1946* (Columbia 46337). Two CDs.
  The original trio and quartet (Goodman, Wilson, Krupa, Hampton) also in good form on airchecks recommended in big band section below.

BOBBY HACKETT

- *Jazz in New York—1944* (Commodore 7009). LP, C, CD.
  Hackett's golden cornet is heard with Lou McGarity and Ernie Caceres. He's also with a Miff Mole group. Muggsy Spanier's Ragtimers are here, too. Pee Wee Russell is in all three groups.

LIONEL HAMPTON

- *The Complete Lionel Hampton, 1937–1941* (Bluebird 6-5536). Six LPs.
  May also be on CD now. If not, it should be. Dozens of great Swing Era players sit in with the never-say-stop-swinging vibes champion.

Recommended Recordings

COLEMAN HAWKINS

- *Giants of the Tenor Sax* (Commodore 7003). LP, C, CD. With Roy Eldridge and Benny Carter.
- *Classic Tenors* (Flying Dutchman 10146). LP. Also tracks by Lester Young. His famous *Body and Soul* solo is on *Coleman Hawkins 1939–1940* (Classics 634), CD, and on Bluebird 65717, LP, C, CD. And elsewhere too.

BILLIE HOLIDAY (TEDDY WILSON)

- *The Golden Years, Vols. 1–2* (Columbia 21 and 40). Three LPs each volume.
- *The Quintessential Billie Holiday, Vols. 1–9* (Columbia 450987, 460060, 460820, 463333, 465190, 466313, 466966, 467914, 47031). Nine CDs. Great, unpretentious music that delineated and ennobled the Swing Era. Innumerable superb players including stars of the Basie, Ellington, Calloway, and Goodman bands. Holiday at her best.

MEL POWELL

- *The World Is Waiting* (Commodore 543). LP.
  Vigorous Powell piano and "Shoeless John Jackson" (Goodman) demonstrates what hot jazz improvisation is all about on *The World Is Waiting for the Sunrise*. Also several fine Joe Bushkin recordings.

DJANGO REINHARDT

- *Djangologie, Vol. 2* (Swing 8424-26). Two CDs.
- *Swing in Paris 1936–40* (Affinity 1003). Five CDs.
- *Swing From Paris* (AVs 5070). CD.
- *Django Reinhardt and the American Jazz Giants* (Prestige 7633). LP.
  Django admirers with sufficient funds will also want the seven-volume set *Djangologie* (Swing 54026).

PEE WEE RUSSELL

- *Jack Teagarden/Pee Wee Russell* (Original Jazz Classics 1708). LP.
  Pee Wee with James P. Johnson, also with Max Kaminsky and Dicky Wells. Teagarden's group includes Ben Webster and Rex Stewart. Russell is a prominent soloist on other recordings on this list.

ARTIE SHAW

- *The Complete Gramercy Five Sessions* (Bluebird 7637). LP, C, CD.
  Pianist Johnny Guarnieri also plays harpsichord. Trumpet ace Billy Butterfield is here in muted form. Set includes the rightfully popular *Summit*

Ridge Drive. These delightful small group Shaw recordings easily meet the test of time.

MUGGSY SPANIER

- *The Great Sixteen* (Bluebird 1295). LP. (This music also on *At the Jazz Band Ball* [Bluebird 86752], LP, C, CD.)
  Sixteen 1939 recordings cherished by traditional jazz fans then and now. Great ensemble wallop. Solos by Muggsy, clarinetist Rod Cless, trombonist George Brunies (with his classic singing of *Ugly Chile*). Includes *Someday Sweetheart, Big Butter and Egg Man,* and *Relaxin' at the Touro.* (The CD adds Bud Freeman records and two 1929 Eddie Condon dates including Jack Teagarden.)

JESS STACY

- *Jess Stacy and Friends* (Commodore 7008). LP, C, CD.
  Piano solos including Bix Beiderbecke's Debussy-influenced *Candlelights,* a duet with Bud Freeman, and trio pieces with Muggsy Spanier and singer Lee Wiley.

ART TATUM

- *Classic Piano Solos, 1934–39* (GRP 607). CD. Originally on Decca.
- *Standard Transcriptions* (Music & Arts 673). Two CDs. Piano solos for radio.
- *Art Tatum Masterpieces* (MCA 4019). Two LPs.
  Sixteen solos, eight with group including blues singer Joe Turner, seven by 1944 trio (Slam Stewart, Tiny Grimes). Incomparable, phenomenal pianist, as all these recordings prove.

FATS WALLER

- *Complete Fats Waller, Vols. 1–2* (Bluebird 551, 5575, 5583, 5905). Each volume has two LPs. Some of this music also on various CDs.
- *Fats Waller and His Rhythm: The Middle Years, 1936–1938* (Bluebird 66083). Three CDs.
  There will never be another Fats Waller, a great musician and a great entertainer.

TEDDY WILSON

(See Benny Goodman and Billie Holiday, above. Some of his famous records with Holiday and others are also reissued on Classics CDs numbered 508, 511, 521, 531, 548, 556, 571. More Swing Era Wilson reissued on many CDs.)

LESTER YOUNG

- *Pres at His Very Best* (Emarcy 66010). LP.
  Most of this may be on CD. Great quartet sides, including the marvelous *Sometimes I'm Happy* with Guarnieri, Stewart, and Catlett. Also with a romping Basie sextet including Basie, Jones, Clayton, Wells.
- *Complete Lester Young on Keynote* (Mercury 830920). Two LPs.
- *Giants of the Tenor Sax* (Commodore 7002). LP, C, CD.
- *Giants of Jazz* (Time-Life 13). Three LPs.
  And swing's President is also superb on many of the Holiday-Wilson recordings listed above and Basie big band recordings listed below.

Collections, Various Groups

- *The Complete Commodore Jazz Recordings, Vols. 1–3* (Mosaic 123, 128, 134). Three LPs.
  A total of 63 recordings including some of the greatest made during the Swing Era. Dozens of fine players: Teagarden, Hawkins, Young, Hackett, Freeman, Spanier, Powell, Russell, Eldridge, Chu Berry, Willie "The Lion" Smith, many others.
- *The Complete Blue Note Recordings of Edmond Hall, James P. Johnson, Sidney DeParis, Vic Dickenson* (Mosaic 11). Six LPs, four CDs.
- *The First Esquire Concert* (Limelight 15723). CD.
  Once only on V-Disc. Armstrong, Hawkins, Tatum, Eldridge, Teagarden, Norvo, Hampton, Holiday, Mildred Bailey, other prominent swingers.
- *Swing Is Here: Small Band Swing, 1935–1939* (Bluebird 82180). LP, C, CD.
  A Krupa small group includes Goodman, Eldridge, Chu Berry. Berry also with Manone groups including an exceptional, atypical performance of *When the Saints Go Marching In*. Berigan on three tracks with Gene Gifford. Note: There are twenty-two pieces on the LP but only sixteen on cassette and CD. In the main, unremarkable music, perhaps. But there are some remarkable solos.
- *52d Street Swing: New York in the '30s* (Decca BRD-646). CD.
  Lively small group jazz by Roy Eldridge, Stuff Smith, Jonah Jones, Bobby Hackett, Benny Carter, Pete Brown, Hot Lips Page, John Kirby, scat singer Leo Watson, among others. The Page group includes Buster Smith and two tracks by Sam Price "and his Texas Blusicians" includes Lester Young. Nearly an hour of music from 78rpm recordings.

Big Bands

CHARLIE BARNET

- *Clap Hands, Here Comes Charlie* (Bluebird 6273). CD.
  Twenty-one of this lively band's 1939–1941 recordings.

COUNT BASIE

- *The Complete Decca Recordings, 1937–1939* (GRP 36112). Three CDs.
  Sixty-three records by the first, and greatest, Basie band.
- *The Best of Count Basie* (Decca 170). Two LPs.
  All of these records are on the *Complete Decca* set above.
- *Essential Count Basie, Vol. 2* (Columbia 40835). C, CD. Recorded in
  1939–1940.
  There are other Basie sets from the Swing Era period including some
  taken from live broadcasts. The reader will not be wasting money on any
  of them. As drummer Buddy Rich once said: "Thank God for Basie!"

BUNNY BERIGAN

- *The Complete Bunny Berigan, Vol. 1* (Bluebird 5584), *Vol. 3* (Bluebird
  9953). LPs, Cs, CDs.
  Berigan did not have a great band, but he always had a great trumpet
  soloist. His famous *I Can't Get Started* is on Vol. 1 and has been reissued
  often. The longer version, originally a twelve-inch 78rpm record (like
  Goodman's two-sided *Sing, Sing, Sing* from the same Victor set) is the
  one to hear. Berigan also featured with Tommy Dorsey, listed below.

BOB CROSBY

- *Bob Crosby, 1937 to 1938* (BCC 688). LP, C, CD.
  Fronted by singer Crosby, this was quite a band, different from other popular swing bands because of its New Orleans Dixieland two-beat spirit. Fine
  soloists included Yank Lawson, Billy Butterfield, Irving Fazola, Matty
  Matlock, Eddie Miller, Bob Zurke. Many selections here are by a smaller
  group from the band, "the Bob Cats." The famous duet by bass player Bob
  Haggart and drummer Ray Bauduc, *Big Noise From Winnetka,* is included.

JIMMY DORSEY

- *Contrasts* (Decca 626). CD.
  Recorded 1936–1943. JD's alto saxophone and clarinet playing should
  not be underrated.

TOMMY DORSEY

- *Complete Tommy Dorsey, Vol. 3, 1936–1937* (Bluebird 5560). Two LPs. Bunny Berigan is on eighteen of these pieces, notably on *Marie* and *Song of India*.

DUKE ELLINGTON

- *The Webster-Blanton Years* (Bluebird 85659). Four Cs, three CDs. (Originally Bluebird 5659, three LPs.)
  Sixty-six recordings over a three-year period (1940–1942). There are many other Swing Era recordings of Ellington's orchestra, including studio transcriptions (notably the CD *Take the 'A' Train* [Vintage Jazz Classics 1003]), and even a 1940 concert in Fargo, North Dakota, but the *Webster-Blanton* package is probably the most essential for any Swing Era enthusiast. Or any music enthusiast. This was great music then and is great music now.

BENNY GOODMAN

- *The Birth of Swing, 1935–1936* (Bluebird 90601). Three CDs.
  The records that ushered in the Swing Era. Still fascinating arrangements by Fletcher Henderson, Jimmy Mundy, Edgar Sampson, among others.
- *On the Air 1937–1938* (Columbia 48836). Two CDs.
  Most all of this originally on two LPs, *Complete 1937–38 Jazz Concert No. 2* (Columbia 180). Much more exciting than his studio recordings and the 1938 concert at Carnegie Hall. These airchecks show what the band really sounded like. With superb music by the trio and quartet, too.
- *The Essence of Benny Goodman* (Columbia 47311). C, CD.
  Recommended mainly because of Eddie Sauter's *Clarinet à la King*, a fascinating piece with fine playing by Goodman. Ever mindful of the dancers then, the peerless jazz clarinetist preferred the arrangements of Fletcher Henderson and others to those by Sauter because "you couldn't dance" to some of Sauter's work. Be that as it may, if a CD set containing all of Sauter's pieces for Goodman is produced, get one.

FLETCHER HENDERSON

- *Fletcher Henderson, 1934–1937* (Classics 527). CD.
  The man who did so much to create big band swing music. Includes *Christopher Columbus* and *Stealin' Apples*.
- *Tidal Wave* (Decca GRD-643). CD.
  Includes 1934 recordings of *Down South Camp Meeting* and *Wrappin' It*

Up, pieces later made famous by the Goodman band, and *Shanghai Shuffle.* Buster Bailey featured on clarinet.

WOODY HERMAN

- *Thundering Herds* (Columbia 44108). Three LPs.
  Forty-eight pieces by the First and Second Herman Herds. All of it should be on CD and perhaps will be someday. From the First Herd, one of the greatest of all big bands ever, stirring sides such as *Apple Honey, Bijou, The Good Earth, Everywhere, Northwest Passage, Goosey Gander, Blowin' Up a Storm.* With the Swing Era mainly over, the Second Herd was organized in 1947 and the last selection here, recorded in 1948, written by Jimmy Guiffre to feature three tenor saxophones and one baritone saxophone, is the groovy *Four Brothers.* (These four "brothers" devoted to the sax appeal of Lester Young were Zoot Sims, Herbie Steward, Stan Getz, and Serge Chaloff.)
- *Thundering Herds, 1945–1947* (Columbia 44108). CD.
  Fourteen tracks from the LPs above.

EARL HINES

- *Piano Man* (Bluebird 86750). LP, C, CD.
  Recorded 1939–1942. Five piano solos plus sixteen orchestra tracks including the memorable *Piano Man,* a Hines composition that Gene Krupa translated into his popular *Drummin' Man,* same tune, different words. The last line of the original goes: "Swing it, Fatha Hines!" And that he certainly could do. Like Armstrong, Ellington, Basie, Goodman, Waller, Tatum, and others, Fatha Hines won great admiration for his artistry the old fashioned way: he earned it.

JIMMIE LUNCEFORD

- *Stomp It Off* (MCA 16082). CD.
  Decca records from 1934–1935.
- *Jimmie Lunceford* (Classics 520, 1937–1939), (Classics 532, 1939), (Classics 565, 1939–1940), (Classics 622, 1940–1941). Four CDs.
  It is fashionable for some jazz history writers to belittle Lunceford's band now. More show biz than jazz, they contend. But this was one of the best Swing Era bands, one that was fun to see and hear, eminently danceable, distinctively different, with good section work and a remarkable reed section led by Willie Smith. Lunceford's most important arranger was Sy Oliver, who left the band in late 1939 to make more money writing for Tommy Dorsey, giving the trombonist's band new life.

ARTIE SHAW

- *Begin the Beguine* (Bluebird 82432). LP, C, CD.
  In late 1938, Shaw's *Begin the Beguine* band became immensely popular. It did not compare with several of his excellent later bands but was not without appeal primarily because of the leader's commanding clarinet, as is demonstrated here. His much more interesting 1940 band (*Star Dust, Moonglow*) is included, too.
- *Blues in the Night* (Bluebird 82432). LP, C, CD.
  Records date from 1941–1945. Sidemen include Hot Lips Page, Roy Eldridge, Georgie Auld, Johnny Guarnieri, and many other first class players. (RCA produced seven two-LP sets of his many Bluebird and Victor records entitled *The Complete Artie Shaw* that has much excellent music but at this writing most of these recordings have not been transferred to CD.)

CHICK WEBB

- *Ella Swings the Band, 1936–1939* (MCA 1327). CD.
- *Chick Webb, 1935–1938* (Classics 517). CD.
  No Ella on the second one.

(Author's note: Big band enthusiasts can find much big band Swing Era music reissued on LPs, cassettes, and compact discs. In addition to more recordings by the bands listed above, it is not difficult to find Swing Era music of interest by the orchestras of Harry James, Gene Krupa, Cab Calloway, Andy Kirk, Glen Gray, Lionel Hampton, Will Bradley, Glenn Miller, Ray McKinley, Claude Thornhill, Bob Chester, Freddie Slack, Les Brown, and Benny Carter, among others.)

Index

All songs, movies, and publications are in italics. To avoid any possible confusion, movies and books are identified as such. The additional reading, recommended recordings, and sources sections are not indexed.

Index

Index